Democracy
and Its
Institutions

Democracy
and Its
Institutions

André Béteille

OXFORD
UNIVERSITY PRESS

OXFORD
UNIVERSITY PRESS

Oxford University Press is a department of the University of Oxford.
It furthers the University's objective of excellence in research, scholarship,
and education by publishing worldwide. Oxford is a registered trademark of
Oxford University Press in the UK and in certain other countries.

Published in India by
Oxford University Press
YMCA Library Building, 1 Jai Singh Road, New Delhi 110 001, India

First Edition published in 2012
Oxford India Paperbacks 2017

ISBN-13: 978-0-19-947167-6
ISBN-10: 0-19-947167-3

Typeset in Adobe Garamond Pro 11/14
by alphæta Solutions, Puducherry, India 605 009
Printed in India by Repro Knowledgecast Limited, Thane

For
P.C. Joshi,
T.N. Madan,
and
J.P.S. Uberoi,
Friends and Intellectual Companions

For

P.C. Joshi,

T.N. Madan,

and

J.P.S. Uberoi,

Friends and Intellectual Companions

Contents

Contents

Acknowledgements

F our of the nine chapters of this work have been published previously. Chapter 1, 'The Institutions of Democracy', was published in *Economic and Political Weekly*, vol. 46, no. 29, 2011, pp. 75–84, and Chapter 4, 'Constitutional Morality', in *Economic and Political Weekly*, vol. 43, no. 40, 2008, pp. 35–42. Chapter 6, 'Caste and the Citizen', was published in *Science and Culture*, vol. 77, nos 3–4, 2011, pp. 83–90. Chapter 9, 'Sociology and Ideology', was published in *Sociological Bulletin*, vol. 58, no. 2, 2009, pp. 196–211. They are being republished here with permission from the editors concerned to whom I would like to express my thanks.

I am grateful to Nitasha Devasar for putting the idea of this book into my mind a couple of years ago at a chance encounter at Delhi airport while we were waiting for our flights to be called.

André Béteille
April 2012

Introduction

When I take stock of what I have written over the last fifty years, I am struck by the distance I have travelled since the publication of my first book (Béteille 1965). That work was an empirical and analytical study of a single village which tried to show how the inequalities of caste and class interacted, and how that interaction was illuminated by a consideration of power and politics at the local level. *Caste, Class and Power*, my first book, was written in a social and intellectual climate that has undergone many changes in the last fifty years. As one might expect, my own intellectual concerns have changed in response to those changes.

When I was at work on my first book, the thought of writing critical and reflective essays on the prospects of democracy in the twenty-first century were far from my mind. The economists in the Delhi School of Economics in whose proximity I worked were all concerned with questions of policy in one way or another. This was certainly true of K.N. Raj, the economist whom I admired the most, and even more true of Dr V.K.R.V. Rao who had established the Delhi School of Economics. M.N. Srinivas had a somewhat different conception of his vocation and I shared the belief he held at that time that sociology or social anthropology had little to offer as a policy science. I was struck by the fact that in both French and German, a single word, 'politique' in French and 'Politik' in German, served to cover what was described by two separate, though related, words, 'politics' and 'policy', in English. If one wished to write about politics, as I certainly did, could one remain indifferent to policy?

It should be made clear that, although I have found it increasingly difficult in practice to insulate social analysis from social policy, I still believe that the separation of value judgements from judgements of reality—or 'ought' questions from 'is' questions—is a good principle that should be kept continuously in mind. My sense is that the secular trend of change in sociology in India has been away from the separation of theory and practice to the point that the autonomy of sociology as an intellectual discipline is accepted at best half-heartedly. Someone who wishes to make a case for it has to swim against the current. One reason why sociology continues to fascinate me despite the tedium of its dull routine is the challenge it poses for someone who strives continuously to maintain the separation of facts and values.

When I was beginning my career as a teacher and an author, I did not recognize the snares and pitfalls that would lie in the path of a sociologist who drifts into the role of a public intellectual. With the advantage of hindsight, I can see that something new entered into my way of looking at society and politics when I began to write occasionally for the newspapers. Forty or fifty years ago, unlike now, academics did not write much for the newspapers, and such writing was viewed with some misgiving by their colleagues. I enjoyed writing for the newspapers and did not feel that by doing so I would be compromising my position as an academic. Perhaps a little naively, I felt that such writing had a pedagogic rather than a political function. It enabled me to explain the nature of sociological reasoning to a wider audience than was available in any classroom.

Reaching out to a wider public through popular articles, I felt, was more consistent with the aims of sociology as an intellectual discipline than serving on committees to advise and recommend policies to the government. At any rate, I found it personally more satisfying. I had the example of Raymond Aron, whose work I greatly admired and who combined with consummate ease the work of sociologist and journalist. And talented though many individual economists were, their work as policy advisers or policymakers had little attraction for me.

Although I believed and hoped that only my scholarly writing would influence what I wrote for the newspapers, the influence in fact acted in both directions. The concern for current affairs made increasing inroads into the way in which I thought and wrote my academic work and, particularly, in the choice of problems to which I devoted scholarly attention. In trying to show that current affairs should be treated sociologically, I became increasingly engaged with those affairs.

Through the various ups and downs in my own development, I have tried to remain steadfast in my commitment to what I would like to describe as 'sociological reasoning'. I have published papers on religion as a subject of sociology and on politics as a subject of sociology (Béteille 2009: 184–224). The application of sociological reasoning demands unremitting toil in an endeavour that is for the most part dull, boring, and repetitive. It is, to adapt a phrase from Max Weber, 'a slow boring of hard boards'. But it opens to view a social universe that is rich, complex, and endlessly fascinating.

In this work I have tried to extend my understanding of institutions to certain crucial features of the political domain. My interest at the start of my career was in social morphology rather than in social institutions. I avoided at first questions relating to norms and values that are central to the understanding of institutions. My interest in institutions grew with my growing awareness of the contradiction between the ideal of equality and the practice of inequality in the modern world. I became aware that it is specifically within the framework of the institution that that contradiction could be observed, described, and analysed.

Today when the failure of public institutions has become a staple of conversation among the educated middle classes, it is important to point out that the systematic study of institutions has had a central place in the disciplines of sociology and social anthropology for a very long time. Those two related disciplines have studied institutions of every kind, and not simply the institutions of governance, and they have studied them in a very wide range of societies from the simplest to the most complex. Sociologists have brought to the study of institutions a set of concepts and methods that enable them to carry their discussions a little beyond the observations of common sense. This is not to say that sociologists everywhere adopt a single definition of institutions on which all of them are in agreement. What is common among them is the approach to institutions rather than any single definition of them.

My own systematic work on institutions began with the institutions of science and scholarship (Béteille 2010) rather than with those of government and politics. I began writing about universities for the newspapers before I wrote about them for a more specialized academic readership. As a sociologist, I realized that a university had to be viewed not simply as a centre of learning but also as a social institution. Anyone who is a member of a university must concern himself with the university as a centre of learning; I believe that the sociologist has also the obligation to view it as a social institution.

The discussion of universities as institutions led me to discuss, on a broader canvas, the institutions of civil society. As I have explained in Chapter 1, I view civil society as a set of institutions which represent, as it were, the social as against the purely political side of democracy. In earlier writings I have discussed in some detail the distinctive features of those institutions that constitute the core of civil society. They are, in short form, open and secular institutions that are homologous with the constitutional state and with universal citizenship. In most contemporary societies such institutions co-exist with other institutions such as those of religion and kinship as well as with communities, associations, and networks of interpersonal relations of various sorts (Béteille 2000: 172–97).

The emphasis in this book is on the institutions of the state or institutions closely associated with the working of the state. This has to be seen in the context of current discussions on the failure of the state and on possible alternatives to it in the form of associations and movements of various kinds. The position adopted here is that the constitutional state and civil society are complementary and not contradictory to each other. The institutions of civil society require an effective constitutional framework for their proper functioning and such a framework can hardly be sustained where social movements set themselves continuously against the authority of the state.

The institutions of civil society cannot flourish where the state is monolithic or despotic. The examples of the Soviet Union under Stalin and the People's Republic of China under Mao come readily to mind. But can they flourish in the absence of an effective state that is mindful of its constitutional obligations?

There is much concern the world over about what are described as 'failed states' in parts of Asia and Africa. The United Nations and other international agencies have taken to providing financial and moral support to associations and movements that act in the name of civil society. It is not easy to see in what way a failed state or a state that is on the verge of becoming one can be shored up by support from outside by agencies that will never be required to take responsibility when their support turns into subversion. A nation which sets itself as a democracy should not turn its back on support from outside, but the plain fact is that such support is not always offered in good faith.

Although ideals such as those of equality, liberty, and fraternity are of great value and significance, I have chosen in this work to dwell more on the institutions than on the ideals of democracy. This is due to my bias as a sociologist who feels more at ease with the study of institutions than with reflections on ideals in themselves. The institutions I have chosen for consideration such as legislatures, courts of justice, and political parties are more amenable to observation, description, and analysis than the ideals with which political theorists and philosophers deal. Further, among the various available conceptions of institutions, I have chosen the one which makes it appear most concrete and tangible.

The focus on institutions has this advantage that it enables us to see most clearly the divergence between ideal and practice in the operation of democracy. While it is true that most nations in the contemporary world subscribe to the ideals of democracy, these ideals do not operate in the same way everywhere. It may be said that the failure of democracy in many parts of the world is at the bottom a failure of its institutions. It is only by examining the operation of those institutions that we can hope to understand why democracy has had such an uneven record in the contemporary world.

It is said that dissent is the essence of democracy and that without dissent there is no democracy. But opposition is present in every society. It is only in democracies that opposition is given an institutional form so that the relationship between government and opposition acquires a kind of value and significance that it has in no other political system. This issue has been examined in some detail in the present work.

The failure of democratic institutions is due, in no small measure, to the failure of trust between government and opposition. The life of an institution depends not only on a distribution of rights and obligations but also on a bedrock of trust among its members. This question comes up in several of the chapters in the book, but is addressed specifically in Chapter 5. There I have tried to show how the language of rights adopted from the politico-jural domain tends to undermine the basis of trust in a wide range of institutions from the domestic to the academic domains. What makes it difficult to assess the balance between rights and trust in an institution is that while rights are relatively easy to identify and to assert or to deny, such is far from the case with trust.

An argument that runs throughout the book is that democracy rests on a tension between two distinct principles, the rule of numbers and the rule of law. This argument is presented as clearly as possible in the opening chapter and illustrated with various examples in other parts of the book. If a nation is to function as a democracy, its people must show some regard for each of the two principles, but the balance between them is not struck in the same way in all nations and it is rarely, if ever, a stable one.

Respect for the rule of law is not equally strong or equally deep in all societies. Many Indians, including highly educated ones, easily run out of patience with the procedures of democracy which are an essential part of any constitutional order. The 'voice of the people' has for them a much more immediate and palpable appeal. It is this disjunction that provides the running thread for the distinction that I have tried to address in many parts of the book between 'constitutional' and 'populist' democracy. As I have pointed out in Chapter 6, the colonial rulers of the country believed that democracy was unlikely to survive in India, which they saw as a society of castes and communities rather than a nation of citizens. They have been proved wrong and democracy has become a part of our destiny.

But while this is true, it is also true that there has been a slow but perceptible shift from constitutional to populist democracy in the sixty years since we became a republic. This book will have served its purpose if it creates in the reader some idea of the nature and significance of this shift.

References

Béteille, André. 1965. *Caste, Class and Power*. Berkeley: University of California Press.

————. 2000. *Antinomies of Society*. New Delhi: Oxford University Press.

————. 2009. *Sociology*. New Delhi: Oxford University Press, 2nd edn.

————. 2010. *Universities at the Crossroads*. New Delhi: Oxford University Press.

1

The Institutions of Democracy*

We live in the age of democracy. This means that democracy provides the touchstone by which political actions and processes are judged as beneficial or otherwise. The virtues of democracy as an ideal of social and political life are acknowledged even in regimes that are at least formally monarchical as in countries such as the United Kingdom, the Netherlands, and the Scandinavian kingdoms of Denmark, Norway, and Sweden. It must be pointed out that this has not been so in all places or at all times, and the validity and legitimacy of what have been called 'aristocratic' as against 'democratic' regimes have been widely acknowledged in the past (Tocqueville 1956).

For many the main virtue of democracy is that it gives the common people a place in the sun. It reduces the gap between the rulers and the ruled by restricting the powers of the former and enlarging those of the latter. In a monarchical or imperial regime in the true sense of the term, the common people are subjects and not citizens. The advance of democracy transforms subjects into citizens. It is a paradox of our time that the rights of citizenship are better respected in monarchies such as Britain and the Netherlands than in democracies such as India or Sri Lanka.

* This chapter was previously published in *Economic and Political Weekly*, vol. 46, no. 29, 2011, pp. 75–84.

Democracy is animated by the lofty ideals of liberty, equality, and fraternity. These were the ideals of the French Revolution which inspired people in many countries to challenge the absolutist monarchies of the past. We too invoked them as our nationalist leaders challenged their colonial rulers. After the attainment of independence we inscribed those same ideals in the Preamble to our Constitution, and added to them justice, social, economic, and political.

Political regimes which call themselves democracies or subscribe to democratic ideals and values have in fact emerged under very different historical conditions and assumed diverse forms and modes of functioning. In many European countries, democratic ideals and values grew in response to the oppressive rule of absolutist monarchs. Here again there were differences even between neighbouring countries. In the United Kingdom the slow ascent towards democratic principles and practices began in 1215 with the Magna Carta although, as I have already noted, the steady expansion of the rights of citizenship has not been accompanied by the abolition of the monarchy or, for that matter, the House of Lords. In France, on the other hand, a more dramatic change took place from monarchy to republic in 1789, although France alternated between republic and monarchy (or empire) well into the second half of the nineteenth century.

The idea of democracy came to us with colonial rule. But as Nirad C. Chaudhuri (1951: v) put it memorably, it conferred subjecthood on us but withheld citizenship. The aspiration of Indians to become a nation of free and equal citizens, which was kindled by colonial rule, was given a distinct focus with the formation of a political party, the Indian National Congress, as early as in 1885. That party became the vehicle for the aspirations of the nationalists against their colonial rulers. Their leaders could ask for national independence only by mobilizing the Indian people as a whole against the colonial regime. They found it natural to use the language of democracy in their fight for independence.

Democracy emerged in India out of a confrontation with a power imposed from outside rather than an engagement with the contradictions inherent in Indian society. Those contradictions remained deeply embedded in the Indian social order even as the country opted for a democratic political order on the attainment of independence. They are giving Indian democracy a very different character from democracy in the West which grew and advanced by confronting a succession of internal social contradictions.

In the West, the democratic and industrial revolutions emerged together, reinforcing each other and slowly and steadily transforming the whole of society. The economic and social preconditions for the success of democracy grew along with, and sometimes in advance of, the political institutions of democracy. In India, the political argument for democracy was adopted by the leaders of the nationalist movement from their colonial rulers and adapted to their immediate objective which was freedom from colonial rule. The building of new political institutions took second place, and the creation of the economic and social conditions for the successful operation of those institutions, such as education, health care, and other social services, lagged well behind.

Ministers, legislators, and even judges never tire of speaking of the need to put service to the common man first. It is a habit of speech that was acquired during the struggle for national independence, and now serves as a mantra on all public occasions. The common people themselves are not sure how much they can depend upon those who repeatedly invoke the ideals of democracy in their name. It is in this context that I turn my attention from the ideals of democracy to the actual operation of its institutions.

*   *   *

While much may be said about democratic ideals and values such as those of liberty, equality, and social justice, I focus my attention here on the institutions of democracy. I do so not only because of the intrinsic importance of institutions for the successful operation of democracy but also because they appear to me to be more concrete and tangible as objects of enquiry and investigation.

The term 'institution' has many meanings, as is to be expected of any term that is used so widely and across so many different disciplines ranging from law and political theory to sociology and cultural anthropology (Béteille 2010: 114–33). Even among sociologists the term has at least two different though related meanings. In the first sense, an institution is an enduring group with a distinct identity and with boundaries that mark it out from its environment. In the second sense, it is a pattern of activities that are recurrent, legitimate, and meaningful. Thus, for the sociologist not only the court but also law is an institution; not only the school but also education is an institution; and not only the family but also marriage is an institution. In both senses the institution has to be distinguished from the individual and from acts that are peculiar to particular individuals.

I find it convenient to begin with the institution as an enduring group that outlives its individual members, and then to move on to the regular and recurrent activities that are a part of that group's existence. The advantage with this is that the institution as an enduring group often has a distinct physical identity as, for instance, the school, the court, or the legislature, and this enables us to form a concrete picture of its social identity. It is relatively easy to form a clear picture of the school as an institution before asking whether what goes on in it does or does not correspond to any meaningful form of education. That is the kind of question that we must ask ultimately about our political institutions but it will be useful for a start to form a concrete picture of those institutions in their concrete settings.

As one would expect in a country with the size, diversity, and antiquity of India, there are many different institutions performing a wide range of functions, social, economic, and political. Some of these institutions have their origins very far back in time while others are of more recent origin, although even here, the older of our high courts can trace their origins back to the nineteenth century. In discussing the institutions of democracy, my focus will be not on the institutions that have come down from our ancient or medieval past, but on those that began to emerge from the middle of the nineteenth century onwards. I will thus not have anything to say about the village democracies of the past about whose institutional form or mode of functioning we know little or nothing.

In speaking about the institutions of democracy, I will focus specifically on the political institutions. It has been recognized for nearly 200 years that democracy has a social as well as a political side (Tocqueville 1956). Of particular importance to the operation of democracy are what I have called the institutions of civil society. The weakness of democracy in India is due in no small part to the weakness of the institutions of civil society. But I will not discuss those institutions here, partly for reasons of space and partly because I have written about them in some detail elsewhere (Béteille 2000a: 172–97; Gupta 2005: 437–58).

*   *   *

My treatment of political institutions will be illustrative rather than exhaustive. I will focus on Parliament and the state legislatures, the Supreme Court and high courts, and on political parties. Others may be added to these, but considerations of space do not permit me to do so. At any rate, no one can deny the great importance and value of the institutions I have chosen for discussion here.

Some will no doubt ask why I have chosen only two of the great institutions of governance, the legislative and the judicial, and left out the third which is the executive. This is not because I consider the executive to be less important than the other two but because I believe that a consideration of any two, and a comparison and contrast of them will suffice to present my main argument about the nature and significance of institutions. Moreover, I have elsewhere discussed in some detail the nature and significance of the executive branch of the government (Béteille 1999: 198–230). My discussion there of the distinction between the political and the administrative executives foreshadows the distinction I make here between the rule of numbers and the rule of law in my contrast between the legislature and the judiciary.

I would like to begin with Parliament. This is a natural point of departure not only because of the obvious importance of Parliament as a political institution but also because of its high visibility. Nothing that happens in Parliament remains a secret. From the very beginning, the press and the public were given access to Parliament when it was in session. Today one can see the proceedings in Parliament on television without having to leave one's drawing room. Live telecasts have led to the demystification of Parliament and, as we shall see, to a certain devaluation of it in the public eye.

Parliament enjoys the pride of place among the institutions of democracy. This is particularly true of the Lok Sabha. Its very name, the House of the People, signals its popular and representational character, and it is not without reason that our form of democracy is known as the parliamentary form. It is true that the President is, constitutionally, the head of both houses of Parliament, but for all practical purposes the conduct of the Lok Sabha is the responsibility of the elected members themselves, and they conduct their affairs in public view.

Direct election by the people gives to the members of the Lok Sabha their distinctive democratic legitimacy. The formal composition of the two houses of Parliament and their powers and functions are laid down in some detail in the Constitution of India. In addition to Parliament, we also have the state legislatures whose organization mirrors in many ways the organization of Parliament.

Along with the central and state legislatures, the Supreme Court and the high courts are the other great institutions of democracy. Courts of justice, no matter how high their standing, are of course not unique to democracies. There have been royal courts of justice, and the British set up courts of justice when they began their rule in India. The courts of justice in independent India have continued many of the conventions and practices established under colonial rule and have been criticized, unfairly in my judgement, for being more colonial than democratic. Those who direct their barbs at the Supreme Court for its colonial antecedents tend to forget that our Lok Sabha itself is modelled in more ways than one on the House of Commons in Westminster.

Whereas our legislators are elected, our judges are appointed according to procedures laid down in the Constitution. A judge does not have a constituency in the sense in which a member of

Parliament has one. An elected member of Parliament has a special responsibility towards his constituents. A judge of the Supreme Court has no constituents towards whom he has any special responsibility. The court is not a popular institution in the sense in which an elected legislature is. It is insulated from public pressure and expected to deal even-handedly with government and opposition.

Because of its higher visibility and its more representational character, many believe that it is Parliament rather than the Supreme Court that embodies most fully the spirit of democracy. The Supreme Court is believed to be 'elitist' rather than popular and hence not fully democratic. This reflects the populist as against the constitutionalist concept of democracy. As the populist conception gains ground, the value placed on the institutions of democracy, including Parliament itself, tends to decline.

Democracy rests on a delicate balance between two principles which may be called the rule of numbers and the rule of law. Numbers are important in a democracy at every level. When a person contests an election, he or the party which supports him makes an assessment of the numbers to see that the candidate has a reasonable chance of success. In Parliament or in any legislative assembly, the success of a motion and sometimes even the survival of the government depend on the ability to muster the right numbers at the right time. This is believed by many to require both manipulation and coercion.

The courts are designed to determine what is right and wrong in the light of the Constitution and the laws. Where there is a violation of the law, the courts have to rule against the violators even where they constitute a majority. In our country the courts have a special significance because disregard for the rule of law is very widespread in the public domain. The true significance of the courts of law in a democracy is that people look to them to protect the citizen against the arbitrary use of power by the state and its functionaries. But they also have the obligation to protect individuals and groups from being unjustly treated simply because they are outnumbered. Democracy requires institutions to ensure that the rule of law is not overwhelmed by the weight of numbers.

In discussing these issues it is important to keep in mind the distinction between power and authority. People who have the numbers behind them often seek to impose their power even where they have no authority in the matter. Many persons who believe that they are backed by numbers because of the electoral support that they have won, or for some other reason feel that the prevalent rules and procedures are obstacles that should not be allowed to frustrate the public interest as they perceive it. Rules and procedures are indeed sometimes obsolete or archaic, and when it is in the general interest for them to change, they should be changed. But here again, they cannot be changed instantly and on the spot but only in accordance with established procedure.

In a large, diverse, and disorderly society with an open political system such as ours, it is never easy to settle an issue of immediate or urgent public concern by the counting of heads on the spot. When a few hundred or a few thousand, or even a few lakh persons bring road and rail traffic to a halt, it is not easy to decide whether they or their victims constitute the majority. The rights and wrongs of the issue have to be decided in accordance with the rule of law and not the rule of numbers. Political leaders make commitments under pressure and in the end it is left to the courts to decide whether those commitments are legally and constitutionally valid. When the courts have to intervene again and again in such matters, the relationship between elected legislators and appointed judges comes under strain and the major institutions of democracy become weakened.

We have now entered a season of coalition politics at the centre as well as in several states. Coalition politics has brought home the fact that the calculation of numbers can be of crucial importance even where the numbers are not very large. He who heads a coalition government has to pay close and continuous attention to the numbers he is able to muster. It is well known that many compromises have to be made in the work of legislation simply in order to keep the numbers together. In some states, it is alleged, whole groups of legislators are sometimes taken away to distant and undisclosed destinations so that they do not desert the government in its hour of need. These actions are often on the borderline between what is legally valid and what is not, and rival parties, or even members of the public, move the courts to give a verdict.

* * *

In his much-acclaimed work on the English constitution, Walter Bagehot (1928) remarked that there was a dignified part and an efficient part in that constitution and that it worked well when the two parts were in proper balance. I believe that our own premier institutions of democracy must be submitted to the test of both dignity and efficiency. I will begin with Parliament and then make some brief observations on the state legislatures before moving to the courts of law.

There have been significant changes in the composition and character of the Lok Sabha since it was first constituted sixty years ago. Socially, it is more representative of the population of the country than in the past. Its membership is drawn from a wider range of castes and classes than before. This is perhaps even truer of the state legislatures. These changes have come about mainly through conscious efforts by each and every political party to widen its base of electoral support from one general election to another. The move to enlarge the presence of women through a system of quotas is yet to bear fruit.

The earlier Lok Sabhas appear in retrospect to be 'elitist' not only in their social composition but also in their style of functioning. They included a fair proportion of professional people, particularly lawyers. Many of them were somewhat detached from the rough and tumble of electoral politics. They were able to keep their hands relatively clean even when they had to enter Parliament by contesting elections. It was believed possible to win an election on the candidate's standing in public life.

Winning an election on the basis of one's professional competence and standing has now become difficult if not impossible. Our present prime minister, Dr Manmohan Singh provides a striking confirmation of this. Nobody can question his personal integrity or his professional competence. But he has ventured only once, and that too unsuccessfully, to contest an election for the Lok Sabha.

Not only has the number and proportion of persons with professional experience and competence declined in the Lok Sabha, the number and proportion of those with real or alleged criminal records has increased. The criminalization of politics has entered the Lok Sabha as well as the Vidhan Sabhas. The disclosed assets of the members of Parliament show that at least in one respect, that of wealth, they are far from being representative of the population of a country in which poverty is pervasive and endemic. If one is able to enter Parliament, one's children are unlikely to ever have to live in poverty.

The style of functioning has also changed, although it is difficult to say how far the change in style is related to the change in composition. One may speak of a change from a temperate to an intemperate style. In a democracy, Parliament is the pre-eminent forum for openly expressing dissent and disagreement. In the past, parliamentary debate was conducted in an atmosphere of civility, in conscious or unconscious imitation of proceedings in the House of Commons in London. Even where disagreement was strong, it was tacitly understood that it had to be expressed in parliamentary language.

The tone of civility has all but disappeared from parliamentary debate. Interruptions are frequent and noisy, and it has become a matter of routine for several persons to speak at the same time. Rushing to the well of the house is no longer an uncommon event, and the speaker has a difficult time in maintaining order, and has to adjourn the house repeatedly. Even the Rajya Sabha, where debates are expected to be less acrimonious, has to be adjourned for lack of order. All of this can now be witnessed on television by the general public which is becoming increasingly inured to misconduct in the House of the People.

Perhaps the lowest point in parliamentary disorder was reached during the debate over the Civil Nuclear Agreement in 2008. The government was determined to get the bill passed and the opposition was equally determined to block it. Because some of those on whose support the government relied were against the bill, the numbers on the two sides were not absolutely clear. The government won in the end by a very narrow margin, and there were the usual allegations of horse trading. What was unusual, however, was that three of the members of the main opposition party rushed into the house with a sack full of currency notes which were placed before the speaker as material evidence of the bribe paid by the ruling party to ensure that the motion was carried. The dignity of the house was compromised as it had never been before.

The speaker of the Fourteenth Lok Sabha, himself a distinguished parliamentarian, expressed his frustration and anguish again and again. His repeated admonitions to the members to act with decorum generally went unheeded. We get a vivid picture of his frustration and exasperation from his memoirs published shortly after he ceased to be a Member of Parliament. On 28 February 2008, he said in the House, 'I am sorry I have to say that you are all working overtime to finish democracy in the country.' Some months later he said, 'I can only say that you are behaving in the most despicable manner,' and, again, on the same day, 'The whole country is ashamed of its parliamentarians' (Chatterjee 2010: 171). Parliament may still be a great institution, but its members are no longer great men. How long can a great institution remain great in the hands of small men?

The ordinary legislative business of Parliament proceeds in a desultory manner until some misdeed of the government, real or alleged, is brought to light. The opposition then pounces on the government and demands an immediate explanation on the floor of the house. The treasury benches try at first to take evasive action, but the opposition remains persistent. The obduracy of the treasury benches is matched by the vehemence of the opposition. The television channels seize their opportunity for breaking news, and lure members of Parliament into their studios where the debates reproduce the disorder of the debates in Parliament.

It is not at all my argument that the demands of the opposition are always unreasonable or that the government never has a reason for refusing to concede those demands. In the noise and disorder generated in Parliament over scandalous misconduct by someone somewhere, it becomes difficult to decide on the merits of the individual case. But the long-term effect of continuous discord and disorder within Parliament is an erosion of public trust in the institution itself.

The successful operation of Parliament as an institution depends on a measure of trust in the fairness of the system by both government and opposition. Here, increasingly each side seems to believe that the other side can act only in bad faith and never in good faith. Perhaps there is a failure of political imagination on both sides. The ruling party finds it hard to imagine having to vacate the treasury benches to make room for its opponents; and the opposition party finds it hard to imagine what it will have to face after it has secured its place on the treasury benches.

The disorder in Parliament detracts not only from its dignity but also from its efficiency. Parliament has to be repeatedly adjourned, sometimes for only a few hours, and sometimes for a few days. Anxiety over a possible boycott of Parliament during the budget session has grown over the years. It has been calculated that 'Out of 1738 hours and 45 minutes, the fourteenth Lok Sabha wasted 423 hours because of disruptions and adjournments due to disorderly scenes' (Chatterjee 2010: 160). This does not necessarily mean that during the hours when it was allowed to work, it always worked in an efficient or business-like manner.

Recently a whole session of Parliament was lost because a determined opposition demanded an enquiry by a Joint Parliamentary Committee which the government was not prepared to concede. It was prepared to have the matter examined by the Public Accounts Committee instead. Even informed citizens are not always able to understand what such differences signify for dealing with the matters on hand. Increasing numbers of them are coming to the view that our legislators are less interested in the designated business of legislation than in settling scores among themselves. There are serious worries about the loss to the exchequer caused by recurrent stalemates in Parliament.

The ordinary legislative business of Parliament proceeds in a desultory fashion. What should be debated in the full house is increasingly left to committees to do. This becomes to some extent unavoidable when the business of legislation expands. Passing the burden of important business on to committees takes care of the requirements of efficiency up to a point. It is regrettable nevertheless that Parliament is no longer able to meet the high expectations of it that were created in the wake of independence, and that its members now spend so much of their time in disputes that appear to be both endless and fruitless.

The Supreme Court has held its place in the public esteem rather better than the Lok Sabha. Despite the occasional allegation of financial impropriety, our judges are still regarded as being on the whole learned, high-minded, and dutiful in contrast with legislators, ministers, and civil servants. The higher courts of justice are smaller, more compact, and more purposeful than the legislatures. They are also better insulated from popular pressure.

A person from any class or community may seek election to Parliament. He may be a peasant, an artisan, or a man with only five years of schooling and still take an active part in parliamentary debate. The appointment of judges is confined to the middle class, and that too, to the upper levels of it. The legal profession is described as a learned profession, and lawyers and judges have an elevated position in society by virtue of their education and occupation. Where the middle class is very small, as it was in India until recently, the higher judiciary stands out from the rest of society. There are pressures now to make the judiciary more representative in terms of caste and community, but it is difficult to visualize a judiciary whose members belong in equal proportions to every social class or stratum.

Judges disagree with each other although these disagreements are not on party lines or not expected to be on party lines. The chief justice has no authority to issue a whip to ensure conformity with his own judgement. When he finds himself in a minority, all he can do is to record a dissenting judgement. Judges express their disagreement in judicial prose and not by shouting at each other or brandishing their fists in open court. And generally speaking, judges are less eager to appear on television than members of Parliament.

Judicial prose is learned, not to say recondite, and at least in India it tends to be prolix. Two or three judges often write separate judgements even when their opinions are substantially the same, and they tend to write at great length. Judicial deliberation and judicial composition take time. As a result, cases remain unattended for months and years.

The law's delay has caused worry to ordinary persons in many places and in many ages, but it seems to have acquired pathological dimensions in India today. This is partly because aggrieved parties are rarely satisfied with the verdict of the lower courts and seek to go on appeal to the higher ones. When a particular party does not want an early decision, he can engage a counsel who is skilled in the art of securing adjournments. It is sometimes suspected that there is collusion between lawyers and judges in expediting or delaying a hearing.

While the law's delay affects large numbers of persons, it does not affect them equitably. As I have indicated, some might benefit from it while others suffer. Indian society is a highly stratified one, and some can bear more easily than others the costs in both time and money of a protracted judicial process. It is natural for those who get entangled in litigation for no fault of theirs to feel that they are the victims rather than the beneficiaries of the courts. Thus, while the court is no doubt an institution, some might question how far it acts as a democratic institution in upholding the principle of equality in its actual practice.

I have so far described and compared Parliament and the Supreme Court. This is only the first step in the understanding of the institutions of democracy. A second and more difficult step would be to examine the relationship between them. They are assigned distinct spheres of operation, but they are expected to work in harmony. There is a wide gap between the expectation and the reality. The question is not simply whether the gap is particularly wide in India today, but whether it is growing wider.

There are various reasons—personal, professional, and others—for friction between Parliament and the Supreme Court. The exclusive jurisdiction claimed by the one is not always recognized as being exclusive by the other. Underlying all of this is the tension between the two irreducible principles of democracy to which I have referred more than once, the rule of numbers and the rule of law. That tension, carried beyond a certain point, may erupt into the kind of disorder that calls for the suspension of the institutions of democracy either for the time being or for good.

*   *   *

Apart from the institutions of the state, such as the legislative and the judicial ones, political parties play an important part in a democracy. Our party system has acquired a distinctive character as the number of parties has increased steadily during the sixty years since independence.

At the time of independence, the Congress party held a unique position as the party of the nationalist movement. Its main adversary, the Muslim League lost its significance in India with the partition of the country. The Hindu Mahasabha underwent several transformations before emerging as the Bharatiya Janata Party, now the principal adversary of the Congress party. The proliferation of parties has given a distinctive character to political alliances in India. It has made those alliances indispensable and at the same time volatile.

There are various reasons behind the proliferation of parties in India. It is a large country with a very diverse population and a tradition of cultural and social pluralism. There are parties and associations representing all shades of ideological orientation from the extreme left to the extreme right. There are secular parties and 'pseudo-secular' ones. In India no party is prepared to disown secularism, and hence when a party is denounced by its adversary for not being secular, it labels the adversary as 'pseudo-secular'.

There are regional parties such as the Asom Gana Parishad, the Telugu Desam Party, and the Dravida Munnetra Kazhagam which have specifically regional interests. But every regional party has an eye on the centre if only because of the concessions it hopes to secure from it. Likewise, a national party, or a party which expects to hold office at the centre seeks to maintain a regional presence and to secure alliances with regional parties at the centre as well as in the states. An alliance partner which is strong only in its own region does not always act consistently in the state and at the centre.

The number of parties increases when an existing party splits into two or more parties. Splits have been quite common in political parties in India. A party may split because of differences in ideology or because of the clash of personal interests and ambitions. In India, the latter is the more important factor, although those who bring about a split always invoke some point of principle as their reason. Politicians have personal ambitions everywhere, but it is only in some countries that personal ambition prevails so frequently over loyalty to the party. It is difficult to say whether this is due to the strength of personal ambition or the weakness of the party as an institution.

Not only personal ambition, but loyalty to family, kin, and community may also override loyalty to the party. The institutional requirements of a modern political party concerned with democratic governance are different from those of groups based on kinship, caste, and community. The shifting alliances among political parties that are a conspicuous feature of the Indian political scene are often governed by the personal loyalties of leaders and their followers.

Is every political party an institution in the sense in which I have been using the term? Here it is important to distinguish between party and faction. Factions have existed since time immemorial, and the Indian soil is congenial to their growth. The political party is of much more recent origin, and it came into being in the political environment created by colonial rule. The oldest political party in the country, the Indian National Congress was created at the initiative of a British civil servant, Allan Octavian Hume.

A leading student of the subject has defined factions in terms of the following five attributes: (i) a faction is a conflict group; (ii) a faction is a political group; (iii) a faction is not a corporate group; (iv) faction members are recruited by a leader; and (v) faction members are recruited on diverse principles (Nicholas 1965). Factions and parties are based on different organizational principles, and where the faction is strong, the party tends to be weak.

As an institution, the party is expected to have a longer span of life than a faction. It is expected to outlive its current members while still retaining its name, its identity, and its basic structure. An important requirement of institutional continuity is the replacement of existing members by new ones according to a distinct set of principles. New members may be inducted by election or by appointment. These are both valid and legitimate principles in a democracy, depending on the nature and functions of the institution. As we have seen, members of Parliament are elected while judges of the Supreme Court are appointed. The conditions of eligibility in the first case are political and in the second case they are professional.

There is a third way in which succession may be ensured, and that is through genealogical connection, in other words, through ties of kinship and marriage. Monarchs are not elected or appointed, they select themselves by virtue of birth. Selection for leadership by birth is a very widespread political practice in India and other South Asian countries. The practice is so widespread as to appear to many to be a principle.

It is to some extent natural for someone growing up in the home of a politician to be attracted to politics just as someone growing up in a medical family may be attracted to the medical and someone in a legal family to the legal profession. But in a society and in an age in which individual ambition counts for something, one may follow one's own aptitude and choose a career for oneself. In India there is a general tendency for young men to be guided by the family in the choice of a career. The genealogical route is followed by default where other criteria of selection are not strictly required. And it is of course much easier to adopt politics as a career without any specialized training than it is to adopt a career in a profession requiring long and arduous training.

The value placed on family and kinship is much stronger in India than it is in countries such as Britain and France where the institutions of democracy based on open and secular principles have had a longer life and a clearer definition. It is not that there have not been political families in those countries, but in general political institutions have been better insulated from the demands of family and kinship. This is because kinship there is not regarded by people in general as the natural route to political office.

Millions, if not hundreds of millions, of Indians believe that when a political leader passes away, particularly when this happens unexpectedly, he should be succeeded by his son, his daughter, his wife, or even his daughter-in-law. We will fail to understand the weakness of the party as an open and secular institution if we ignore the pressure for genealogical succession characteristic of our social order.

One of our leading journalists and political commentators, Inder Malhotra (2003) has provided a well-documented account of dynastic politics on the subcontinent. He has pointed out that dynastic politics in India is not confined to the Congress party or to what has come to be described as the first family in the country. He has documented the rise of what he calls 'midi' and 'mini' dynasties in various states. These dynasties aim to secure control not only over the party but also over the government. Dynastic control over a party loses its strength where the party has little prospect of forming a government.

* * *

I have in the foregoing drawn attention to the maladies by which what I consider to be the basic institutions of democracy are beset in India today. My objective is not to argue that these institutions have become dispensable or valueless and that we should try to build a new and more vibrant form of democracy in which people govern themselves by creating new social movements and new associations. On the contrary, it is because I believe in the great importance of those institutions and the need to maintain them in some order that I have drawn attention to their current failings. Elsewhere, I have drawn attention to the distinction between constitutional and populist democracy (Chapter 4 in this volume). We started on independence to create a constitutional democracy, and I believe that we adopted the right path and should not be diverted from it.

If we look back on what we had expected of our democratic institutions at the time of independence, we are bound to be disappointed. In his closing speech to the Constituent Assembly, Dr Ambedkar had expressed hope for the future but he had also warned against complacency (*CAD* 1989, X–XII: 978). The 'grammar of anarchy' against whose revival he had warned, far from dying down, has acquired new legitimacy from various sources. But if we look around and view developments in our neighbouring countries and further afield in the countries which have also become independent and self-governing, we cannot but see the difference that democratic institutions have made to India's vast population. Some have benefited substantially from them although others, constituting perhaps the majority, have benefited only marginally.

Our party system has failed in many important respects, but we still have a plurality of parties which are able to express divergent views in the legislatures and outside. Parties are able to articulate divergent views in a manner that is more reasonable, more coherent, and more constructive than the voices raised in demonstrations, rallies, and other evanescent gatherings that are the staple of populist as against constitutional politics. And if we are bedevilled by the multiplicity of parties, it is well to remember that a system with many parties is still a democracy which a system with one single party is not.

The institutions of which I have spoken—Parliament, the Supreme Court, and even the political parties—stand as bulwarks against the dangers by which democracy is threatened, particularly in those countries where commitment to its basic principles is weak. Without those institutions, neither respect for the rule of law nor care for the interests of the disadvantaged would be sustained for long. The two dangers by which democracy is threatened in many countries are anarchy and the abuse of power (Béteille 2000b). They threaten it from opposite sides, but have ultimately the same effect.

The country experienced a period of authoritarian rule during the Emergency of 1975–7 when the abuse of power became widespread and almost a matter of routine. The due process of law was disregarded; leaders of opposition parties were put in jail; the courts remained silent and complicit. The Emergency took a toll on the opposition, but, what is more important, it discredited the Congress party in the eyes of the people and to some extent even in the eyes of some of its own reflective members. Few people today, irrespective of the party they support, look back on the Emergency with satisfaction or pride. The Emergency did not abolish the institutions of democracy, but by subduing them, it created at least for a while a deeper awareness of their value.

In retrospect, the Emergency was relatively mild, and it did not last very long. The person who imposed it herself brought it to an end by calling for elections. In the fitness of things, she lost the elections and her party had to take its place on the opposition benches. Mrs Gandhi certainly succeeded in bending the institutions of democracy to her will, but only to some extent. She has been described repeatedly as a dictator and a despot, but compared with real dictators such as Hitler, Stalin, or Mao, she was at best a half-hearted dictator.

What made Mrs Gandhi a half-hearted dictator was not so much any trait of personal character as the institutional environment in which she had made a place for herself. She may have despised the legislators, the judges, and even the members of her own party as individuals, but she could not cast out of her political imagination the institutions they served and that stood above them (Dhar 2000).

India has a large and articulate body of public intellectuals comprising journalists, lawyers, social scientists, and many others. Some of them enjoy only a local or regional reputation while others are known nationally or even internationally.

Public intellectuals play a very significant role in a democracy. At their best they act as the conscience-keepers of the nation. But many of them, at least in India, are inclined to adopt vehement if not sensationalist modes of expression which tend to obscure instead of clarifying public issues. Even reckless attacks on the authorities do not generally entail significant costs in India at least in comparison with other countries such as China, Iran, or the Soviet Union during its ascendancy. This leads many public intellectuals to position themselves, almost as a matter of routine, against the authorities and on the side of that amorphous and indefinable body known as the people and now, increasingly as 'civil society'. As a result, the deeper roots of political failures remain unattended.

Here I would like to make a distinction between individual misconduct and institutional failure. My main interest as a sociologist is in the latter and not the former. Our legal system has procedures for dealing with individual misconduct. Admittedly, those procedures do not always work fairly or expeditiously. But, frequent and repeated recourse to agitations and demonstrations brings us close to the grammar of anarchy. They cast doubts on the efficacy of the prescribed procedures and undermine their regulatory capacity.

No public institution can work effectively where there is a general failure of trust and where that failure is expressed openly, repeatedly, and stridently. There is a rising current among our public intellectuals of emancipationist and antinomian rhetoric. In this kind of rhetoric the target of attack shifts from particular individuals to the institutions they serve, and finally to the whole institutional order of society, including the institutions with which I have dealt. Parliament, the Supreme Court, and the party system have all begun to reveal deficiencies that had at first remained concealed. Those deficiencies should be brought to light by public intellectuals and criticised, but constructively and not destructively. Relentless antinomian assaults that undermine public confidence in them lead to a weakening of democracy and not its strengthening, even when those assaults are made in the name of the highest ideals of democracy.

*   *   *

The institutions of democracy have not served the people of India as well as they were expected to. They have repeatedly and persistently acted against the spirit of democracy. This has been pointed out time and again by the well-wishers of those institutions as well as their adversaries. The reasoned criticism of public institutions, no matter how severe, is one thing; their thoughtless and wilful denigration is another. It does not appear right to me to argue as if our economic, social, and political advance in the last sixty years owed nothing to them.

It is of the essence of democracy to allow open criticism of its institutions not only in Parliament, but also outside it, in the press and in meetings and associations of various kinds. Civil disobedience too has a legitimate place in a democracy. But the greatest exponent of it, Mahatma Gandhi always maintained that the civil disobedient must be prepared to submit his own conduct to stricter moral scrutiny than the ordinary citizen. Moreover, as Dr Ambedkar had pointed out in the Constituent Assembly, the entire context of civil disobedience had changed with the change from a colonial state to an independent nation with a republican constitution (*CAD* 1989, X–XII: 978).

Not all the protests, demonstrations, and rallies organized against the government or in defiance of it correspond to Mahatma Gandhi's idea of civil disobedience, or to anybody's idea of it. Many of them, including some that are organized in the name of civil society, are anything but civil.

Civil society has to play an active role in a democracy. But today we cannot ignore the fact that what are called civil society movements differ very much among themselves in character and composition, and have very diverse political agendas including some that are not only antithetical to the spirit of democracy but are very peculiar in their demands. Perhaps we ought to take a tolerant view and allow the public expression of views that we know are unlikely to lead anywhere at all.

Should we mistrust all civil society movements simply because some of them might lead to the disruption of public institutions? That would be to throw the baby out with the bathwater. Which of the movements organized in the name of civil society advance the objectives of democracy and which ones subvert them are questions on which each citizen must form his own judgement, and this is what democracy allows and, indeed, encourages its citizens to do.

No matter how much we value social movements for the part they play in keeping both government and opposition on their toes, they cannot be a substitute for the institutions of democracy. We have to distinguish between social movements that act within the framework of democratic institutions and those that have to act because such a framework does not exist, or exists only in name. In India some leaders of popular movements speak and act as if no such framework exists, or as if democracy can be established only by dismantling what exists.

In India a framework of democratic institutions not only exists but has acted as a shield against the most menacing threat to democratic rule, which is military rule. Many well-meaning social activists believe that once the corrupt government and the equally corrupt opposition have been put aside, a new and incorrupt leadership will automatically emerge from among the people by a spontaneous act of self-generation, a kind of socio-political parthenogenesis. This might happen in the realm of fantasy, but it is not what generally happens in the real world.

When an existing government is overthrown by a popular upsurge, the responsibility for forming a new government sometimes falls on the military. This is the likely outcome when the opposition is not constituted as an institution. If we look around in our neighbourhood and beyond to the countries of West Asia and North Africa, we will find many examples of this. Where the institutions of democracy are feeble and unformed, the army is a natural candidate for taking over the government of a country. Where those institutions are strong and well regarded, the army is likely to stay in its place.

If the army has shown little inclination to take over the burden of government in India, it is in no small measure because it has been on the whole kept in its place by Parliament, by the Supreme Court, and by the political executive. No military man has ever been the president or prime minister of independent India, and so far as I can recall none has even been the defence minister. The subordination and the accountability of the army to the civilian authorities are tacitly acknowledged by all parties, even by those who never miss an opportunity to denigrate those very institutions.

In other countries where those institutions have at best a fitful existence it might appear natural for the army to step into the vacuum created by a popular upsurge. This is because the army appears to many people to be the only institution that is modern, secular, and progressive and that can hold the country back from a descent into chaos. In countries such as Egypt and Tunisia people have little to choose between being ruled by the army and living in a state of continuous disorder. In India we do have a choice but many of our public intellectuals appear unmindful of what the institutions of democracy have enabled us to escape.

We must not underestimate the significant part that the army has played in many countries in the modernization of society. Egypt offers a good example. Few will deny the social and economic advances made by that country between King Farouk's time and the present. But those advances were made by a regime headed by three successive military men: Nasser, Sadat, and Mubarak. I have been told by persons who understand and sympathize with Pakistan's predicament—Americans, Indians, and even some Pakistanis—that Indians do not understand what Pakistan owes to its army. We must not treat lightly what we owe to our democratic institutions for enabling us to manage our political affairs without incurring too many debts to our army.

References

Bagehot, Walter. 1928. *The English Constitution*. London: Oxford University Press.

Béteille, André. 1999. 'Experience of Governance', in R.K. Dar (ed.), *Governance and the IAS*, New Delhi: Tata McGraw-Hill, pp. 198–230.

———. 2000a. *Antinomies of Society*. New Delhi: Oxford University Press.

———. 2000b. 'Anarchy and Abuse of Power', *Economic and Political Weekly*, vol. xxxv, no. 10, pp. 779–83.

———. 2010. *Universities at the Crossroads*. New Delhi: Oxford University Press.

Chatterjee, Somnath. 2010. *Keeping the Faith*. New Delhi: HarperCollins.

Chaudhuri, Nirad C. 1951. *The Autobiography of an Unknown Indian*. London: Macmillan.

Constituent Assembly Debates (CAD). 1989. *Official Report*. New Delhi: Government of India, vols X–XII.

Dhar, P.N. 2000. *Indira Gandhi, the 'Emergency' and Indian Democracy*. New Delhi: Oxford University Press.

Gupta, Dipankar (ed.). 2005. *Anti-Utopia: Essential Writings of André Béteille*. New Delhi: Oxford University Press.

Malhotra, Inder. 2003. *Dynasties of India and Beyond*. Delhi: Harper Collins.

Nicholas, Ralph W. 1965. 'Factions: A Comparative Analysis', in Michael Banton (ed.), *Political Systems and the Distribution of Power*, London: Tavistock, pp. 21–61.

Tocqueville, Alexis de. 1956. *Democracy in America*. New York: Alfred Knopf, 2 vols.

2

Government and Opposition

The successful operation of democracy is the responsibility as much of the opposition as of the government. In the parliamentary form of democracy, which India adopted after independence, government and opposition mimic each other to a considerable extent. People expect an alternation of the same persons or groups of persons between government and opposition in course of time. Those who are in opposition now can expect to be in government when their turn comes; and those who are in government now can expect to be in opposition in their turn. It is a failure of political imagination for the same group to expect to remain in either government or opposition for all time and to act on that presumption.

Discontent, dissent, and opposition are perennial features of social and political life everywhere and in all times. But they are dealt with differently in different societies, ranging from pragmatic tolerance to ruthless suppression. Disagreement and opposition were endemic in agrarian communities where resistance to authority was generally diffuse and passive (Scott 1985). Where opposition was organized, such opposition was sporadic and intermittent rather than continuous. In modern totalitarian systems, opposition is driven underground (Figes 2007) until it bursts out in acts of violence and destruction.

Democratic regimes are distinctive if not unique in the way in which they perceive opposition and deal with it. In such regimes, dissent and opposition are regarded as reasonable and legitimate, and not merely expected, features of life. Those who are committed to democracy in the sense in which I am using the term are mistrustful of regimes in which opposition is absent, particularly when their leaders say that since the authorities take care of the well-being of the people as a whole there is really no need for opposition. Such authorities regard dissent in any form as the work of mischief makers. This has been the case in the twentieth century with regimes that describe themselves as 'people's democracies' or 'people's republics'.

Those who commend the virtues of such democracies or republics often do so from their anxiety over the confusion and disorder that prevail in nations that allow the free and open expression of dissent. But the expression of dissent need not necessarily lead to confusion and disorder, although it cannot be denied that the possibility of that is always present. The adoption of the democratic system is a wager based on trust in those who are opposed to the authorities. The absence of this trust leads in the end to either anarchy or authoritarian rule (Béteille 2000). In many countries today, democracy has to pursue an unsteady course between those two unhappy alternatives.

The success of democracy depends not only on recognizing the opposition as legitimate, but also on its being given an institutional form. The institutionalization of opposition is one of the most significant innovations of democracy and acquires its clearest expression in the parliamentary version of it. What it does is to give a distinct structure to the relationship between government and opposition by differentiating the one from the other and assigning each its specific place in the political system. In this process the political system itself acquires a clearer definition in the larger social system.

As the political system acquires a clearer definition through the regular and systematic interaction between government and opposition, politics emerges as a distinct and specialized field of activity, first as a vocation and then as a career. The moralist tends to look down on the professional politician, but the social theorist cannot deny the significant part he plays in every democratic system. The rise of the professional politician is a relatively recent phenomenon in human history and it has much to do with the way in which democracy has developed through the structured relationship between government and opposition.

* * *

The institutionalization of opposition has been a complex process with many twists and turns. It has not followed the same course everywhere. Each country adopted its own course depending on the particular historical and social conditions prevalent in it. Britain provides a very good example because of its early start and because of the great influence it exercised through its far-flung empire. After India came directly under the crown in 1858, the government tolerated and even encouraged the adoption of some of the conventions and practices of regulated opposition already established in Britain. It was under colonial rule that Indians first learnt about the significance of the opposition as an institution although the opposition was not given by any means the same liberties in the colonies as in the home country.

The emergence of the political party as an institution has played a crucial part in shaping the relationship between government and opposition as a distinctive feature of democratic political systems. It is through the party system that the alternation between the two became established as a regular, expected, and acceptable part of democracy. The party in office accepted its replacement by the party in opposition in the expectation that it would be asked to form the government again in the future. The party system gave opposition a focus and at the same time moderated its excesses.

The party emerged as a political institution only in the nineteenth century. It gradually displaced other forms of political association such as the political club, the caucus, and the faction. As an institution the party has a distinct identity with distinct boundaries that mark it out from other associations of its own kind or of other kinds. It is an enduring group that outlives its individual members and maintains its identity over time. It is in this sense that a party is an institution whereas a faction is not, but this is a point on which I will have more to say later. The club is an institution (Hsu 1963), but it is not a specifically political institution with distinct political aims and objectives such as a party is expected to have.

Britain was one of the first countries in which the political party began to acquire its modern institutional form. This happened sometime between 1832 and 1885 with the adoption of three reform Acts which successively extended the franchise (Norton 1981: 26–46). The rivalries of the Whigs and the Tories came to be replaced by the contest between the Liberals and the Conservatives as they organized themselves into modern political parties adapted to the demands of large electorates. A third political party, the Labour Party, came into being at the turn of the twentieth century. Our first political party, the Indian National Congress, was established through the initiative of a British civil servant working in India.

The alternation of parties between being in government and in opposition is best seen in two-party systems although the same principle may be seen at work in systems with three or more parties. Here again, Britain provides a very good starting point because for most of the time since the middle of the nineteenth century it has had in effect a two-party system with the alternation first between the Conservatives and the Liberals, and then between the Conservative and the Labour parties. The political leaders who led the movement for independence in India were fully familiar with the working of democracy in Britain through the alternation of parties. But the relationship between government and opposition acquired a different colour in this country because the social and historical context in which it had to make a place for itself was substantially different.

The relationship between government and opposition became further defined with the development, alongside the party system, of the cabinet system of government. Here again developments in Britain foreshadowed developments in many countries including, of course, India. The leader of the opposition has come to be recognized as an important functionary with a defined role and defined perquisites of office. Just as one party selects the prime minister through its own conventions and procedures, so too its counterpart selects the leader of the opposition through similar conventions and procedures. Those conventions and procedures, which evolved over a long span of time in Britain, have undergone significant alteration while being adapted to the Indian political environment.

Madhu Dandavate, a teacher of political science who served briefly as a member of the Union cabinet, maintained that the leader of the opposition 'should be able to perform his duty as effectively as performed by the Prime Minister or a Chief Minister. The most important function of the leader of the opposition is not only to seek consent but to co-ordinate the activities of the members of the opposition' (Dandavate 1996: 60). It is in particular his responsibility to safeguard the privileges of the House and its individual members.

In a smoothly working parliamentary system, the leader of the opposition can reasonably expect to become head of the government in the future. It is, naturally, his hope that he will not have to wait very long. Tony Blair, one of the longest serving prime ministers of post-War Britain, has given a vivid account of this expectation and its fulfilment. Like any ambitious young politician he had harboured hopes of being called to high office some day. The opportunity came his way when the leader of the opposition, John Smith, died prematurely in 1994. After successfully contesting for the post left vacant by Smith, Blair knew that it would be only a matter of time before he became prime minister, which in fact he did within three years.

Blair has discussed that phase in his political career in a chapter entitled 'The Apprentice Leader' (Blair 2010: 30–63). His account makes it clear, as many others did before it, that at least in Britain, one does one's apprenticeship for the office of prime minister by serving as leader of the opposition. In that capacity the politician not only learns how to demand satisfaction from the government, he also realizes, or ought to realize, what he will have to face as head of the government when others demand satisfaction from him. That realization should serve to moderate the assaults of the opposition on the government.

The expectation of office and the responsibility that goes with it is further developed through the conventions of the shadow cabinet. These conventions have become so well established in Britain as to be virtually an institution. An important task of the new leader of the opposition after he has been chosen is to constitute the group that will act as his shadow cabinet. This will include the shadow chancellor, the shadow foreign secretary, the shadow secretary for defence, and so on. The shadow cabinet acts as a cabinet-in-waiting. Its task is not only to keep the cabinet-in-office under close scrutiny but also to prepare itself for the responsibility of government when it is called upon to take office (Campbell 2007: 3–187).

*   *   *

I have in the foregoing tried to explain the contribution of the party system to the development of a symbiotic relationship between government and opposition. I have dwelt on the example of the British party system because it brings out particularly well the basic features of that relationship. But not all party systems have the same structure, and, even when they do, they may not all function in the same way.

Although the Indian model of democracy was greatly influenced by the British model of it from the inception of the nationalist movement in the nineteenth century till the time of independence in 1947, the evolution of political institutions has since then followed its own distinctive trajectory. In particular, the party system has acquired a shape and a colour that makes it very different from the one in Britain. The role of the opposition, and the relationship between government and opposition, both within and outside Parliament, have acquired distinctive, not to say unique, characteristics in India.

It has been conventional among political scientists to distinguish between two-party and multiparty systems. In a well-known textbook on the subject, Maurice Duverger (1954) took Britain and the United States as examples of two-party systems, and his own country, France, and some other European countries as examples of multiparty systems. But multiparty systems differ greatly among themselves, depending upon the number and variety of parties they have to accommodate. Although India has what is technically a multiparty system, that system is very different from the multiparty systems of France and Germany. This is an important point to which I will return later.

Party systems evolved in the nineteenth century in Europe and the United States, emerging as either two-party or multiparty systems, and occasionally oscillating between the two. The Bolshevik Revolution introduced a genuine innovation by creating and sustaining a one-party system (Pipes 1991: 506–65). The one-party model travelled from the Soviet Union to countries under its shadow in eastern Europe as well as to China and beyond. A variant of the one-party system emerged in Germany under Hitler and in Italy under Mussolini, but neither the Nazi nor the Fascist party lasted very long.

The People's Republic of China is today the best exemplar of a one-party system. Opponents of communist systems will say that China is not a democracy, but that is not how the political leaders of China and perhaps the majority of the Chinese people view the matter. They would say that China is a peoples' democracy which they regard as superior to bourgeois democracies of the kind that prevail in other parts of the world. China and India stand at opposite ends of the spectrum: China has only one single party whereas India has a very large number of parties, so many that it is not always easy to keep count of them.

Where there is only one single party, can we speak of a party system? After all, a system—any system—has to comprise more than one unit, and its character as a system depends upon the interaction between the units which are its component parts. But I believe that it is reasonable, at least under certain conditions, to speak of one-party systems, and that the erstwhile Soviet Union and the People's Republic of China today meet those conditions.

It will not be difficult to argue that the political party enjoys greater prominence in one-party than in two-party or multiparty systems. It will be a mistake to believe that it does so only by creating fear or using terror although it has done both in ample measure.

It has also inspired loyalty and sacrifice in greater measure than any political party in a two-party or multiparty system. The Communist Party in a one-party system has to be treated as a party because large numbers of its members believe that it is a party to which they give their loyalty and support.

The political party, which came into being in the nineteenth century partly if not mainly to articulate dissent and opposition, has been used in the twentieth century and beyond also for suppressing dissent and opposition. The same party can be used successively as a vehicle of dissent and as an instrument for its suppression. The National Socialist Party was used by Hitler first for organizing dissent and, after capturing the state, for suppressing it. This was the case with the Bolshevik Party in Russia (Bullock 1993) and other parties in Europe, Asia, and Latin America which modelled themselves on it.

It is ironical that the political party should occupy such a central place in single-party systems which liberals would regard as totalitarian and not democratic at all. It was Lenin who took the first step to put the party in its commanding position on the Soviet political stage. Lenin's work was carried forward with ruthless efficiency by Stalin who ruled the country through his party continuously for three decades.

Stalin shaped the Communist Party of the Soviet Union into a unique instrument of political control whose dominance extended far beyond the frontiers of his own country. It was he who established the pre-eminence of the party over the government. He held several positions in his long career, but none of them carried the power or the symbolic significance of his position as general secretary of the party which he assumed in 1922 in Lenin's dying months. For a long time he held no official position of any significance except that of the general secretary of the party. He was known in his own country as well as the outside world as the head of the Communist Party of the Soviet Union, in which position he remained until his death in 1953.

Why and how did the party become such a unique instrument for the maintenance of authoritarian rule? Authoritarian rule did not by any means come into being with the emergence of the one-party system in the twentieth century. History offers many examples from

Europe and beyond of absolutist kings and emperors who made short work of dissent and opposition. Louis XIV of France, who said, 'l'état, c'est moi', is a well-known example. Other examples from Europe are Peter the Great of Russia and Frederik the Great of Prussia, and one can find many examples from Asia before the age of political parties.

Both the Bolshevik Party in Russia and the National Socialist Party in Germany were first in opposition before they captured power, through a revolution in the first case and manipulation and intimidation in the second. A single party does not become the sole party all on its own. It acquires its character as a distinct political force by contending with other political parties, dominating them, drastically reducing their power, and then eliminating them. It does not always have to eliminate all its rivals in order to assume effective control over the system. Indeed, it is by contending with these rivals in its early phase of existence that it acquires its own internal coherence and its self-confidence.

The true significance of the single party in a one-party system lies in its role in mobilizing and maintaining popular support for the regime. In the age of democracy, authoritarian rule can claim legitimacy only from popular support, and it is no accident that so many of them call themselves 'peoples' democracies' or 'peoples' republics'. The simple fact is that no regime can be maintained for long without legitimacy, although the basis of legitimacy might differ from one regime to another. In the age of absolutism the monarch sought his legitimacy from the principle of divine right. In the age of democracy legitimacy has to be based on popular support, and the party has become indispensable for creating and maintaining that support, whether in substance or in form.

* * *

Another innovation in the domain of political discourse is the idea of 'partyless democracy'. Although that idea has a very different genesis from the idea of a one-party system, both ideas stress unity and harmony, and view dissent and disunity in a negative light.

However, unlike one-party democracy, the idea of partyless democracy has not acquired any concrete organizational form so that it is difficult to say how it might operate in practice.

It can be said that the idea of 'partyless democracy' is a specifically Indian innovation. In the period after independence it came to be associated with the name of one of the most eloquent political leaders of the country, Jayaprakash Narayan. Simultaneously, he also advocated the idea of *sampurna kranti* or 'total revolution' (Narayan 1978).

Part of Jayaprakash's appeal, particularly for the youth, arose from his courage and dedication, and his rejection of Nehru's offer after independence to join his cabinet. He has been successively a Marxist and a Gandhian, and never seemed to be satisfied with the solutions that people, including himself, offered for India's endless political problems (Narayan 1959; Béteille 2000).

Although he expressed considerable sympathy for 'partyless democracy', Jayaprakash was never sure as to when it could be created or whether it could be created at all. When pressed to the point he would say that partyless democracy was not his immediate aim, but his ultimate aim. He also invoked the authority of Vinoba Bhave and Mahatma Gandhi in support of partyless democracy. He said, 'However, partyless democracy is not a creature of Jayaprakash's wicked mind. It is implicit in Gandhiji's thought and explicit in Vinobaji's *Lok Niti*' (Narayan 1978: 121).

JP's yearning for partyless democracy arose from his growing frustration with the political parties of his time. The ideals of austerity and sacrifice, which had inspired many people during the nationalist movement and of which he himself had been a great exemplar, did not survive the attainment of independence for very long. The political parties became more, and not less, venal and corrupt. Jayaprakash alternated between withdrawal from politics and return to it. He certainly had a great influence on political life, but even at the height of his influence, like Gandhi, he refused to accept political office (Dhar 2000: 223–68, 300–51). Perhaps he yearned for not only a political order without parties but also a social order without politics.

As JP's disenchantment with all political parties, including his own, grew he turned increasingly from the institutions of democracy to social movements for the regeneration of democracy. He placed his hopes especially on the youth and on what he called 'youth power'. When people speak of him today, they do not associate his name with any political party, although he was associated with more than one party in his time, but as the inspiration behind the 'JP movement'. The JP movement did certainly stir things up, but it can hardly be said to have led to any significant moral cleansing. The young men—and they were mostly men—who earned their spurs in the JP movement returned to party politics a little more hardened and a little better prepared for the realities of political bargaining.

It is important to have an institutional mechanism for the expression of dissent. In its absence, dissent tends to remain suppressed until it flows over into movements of protest whose leaders seek to give them a revolutionary colour. The movements create a strong sense of euphoria but also lead to dislocations in civic life. Sooner or later the euphoria disappears and people tire of what has memorably been called 'the grammar of anarchy'. Then there are calls for the restoration of discipline and order, and powerful personalities, usually with military experience, step in to fill the vacuum at the top. We have been fortunate in India that our armed services have not so far played much part in either encouraging or suppressing popular movements. In the end, it may be our institutions of democracy that have, for all their deficiencies and flaws, deterred our men in uniform from harbouring unreasonable aspirations.

JP was of course right in claiming the inspiration of Mahatma Gandhi for his attraction to partyless democracy. Gandhi's disaffection with politics came from a somewhat different source than JP's: for one thing, he had never been attracted by Marxism. Although he had little tolerance for corruption and inefficiency, his mistrust of party politics had deeper moral roots. His idea of the good society was that it was a society based on unity and consensus, and not dissension and conflict. Party politics not only accommodated dissension and conflict, but encouraged them by giving them an institutional form.

Gandhi was a radical in many ways, but not in his conception of the good society.

Gandhi returned again and again to the ideals of the village republic by which he believed public life in India had been governed in the past (Gandhi 1962). On this of course the views of the principal architect of our Constitution, Dr B.R. Ambedkar, were diametrically opposite. Gandhi's communitarian ideals and his commitment to the 'village republics' of the past were expressed again and again in the Constituent Assembly. They still appeal to many people if only because they appear to offer an authentic alternative to the unsatisfactory and unsuccessful experience of western institutional forms.

Jayaprakash turned to the ideals of communitarian politics after his disenchantment with the party system and, indeed, the whole system of parliamentary democracy. While it is true that Jayaprakash, like many Gandhians in the Constituent Assembly, appealed to the alternative held dear by Gandhi, it is doubtful how far Gandhi himself would have endorsed JP's ideas about youth power and total revolution. The nostalgia for the village republics of the past continues till the present day, and no doubt played a part in the promotion of Panchayati Raj institutions down to the time of Rajiv Gandhi.

Not everyone yielded to the idea of the village republic in India. India's leading sociologist in the years following independence, M.N. Srinivas took a sceptical view of it and encouraged others, including myself, to take that idea with a pinch of salt (Béteille 1980). Our knowledge and understanding of Indian communities and of Indian politics have grown enormously since Gandhi's time, and it is difficult to sustain the belief any longer that the Indian village can be made free from dissension and conflict. The question today is how such dissension and conflict can be best addressed, whether by brushing them under the carpet or by creating institutional forms for their orderly expression.

The person who attacked the myth of the village republic most relentlessly was Dr B.R. Ambedkar, and he did it in the Constituent Assembly itself. He first taunted the enthusiasts for the village community, of whom, as I have already indicated, there were many in the Assembly: 'The love of the intellectual Indians for the village community is infinite if not pathetic.' He then turned to those who praised the village for having survived every vicissitude through the ages. 'That they have survived through all vicissitudes may be a fact. But mere survival has no value. The question is on what plane they have survived. Surely on a low, on a selfish level. ... I hold that these village republics have been the ruination of India' (*CAD* 1989, VII: 39). What struck Dr Ambedkar about the village was its pettiness, its narrowness, and its bigotry.

* * *

No doubt the village community was free from the conflict of political parties. But was it free from factional strife?

Factions have been a part of the social and political landscape of India and other countries since time immemorial whereas the political party is an innovation of modern democracy. To some extent, factional politics is displaced by party politics, but not to the same extent everywhere. Factional divisions and conflicts, though present in all societies, do not affect the structure and organization of political parties in all of them equally. The strength of the political party appears to be inversely related to the predominance of factions in the social and political environment. Sometimes factions become so closely intertwined with the life of the party that they threaten to choke the operation of the system.

As I have noted earlier, the faction is not an institution in the sense in which a political party is. As an institution, the party has a charter and a mandate which sets out its aims and objectives. No matter how broad those aims and objectives may be, the party is expected to work towards them whether in government or in opposition. It is another matter that the same party often speaks in a different voice in moving from one side of the house to the other. Despite the rivalries between them, political parties often come to resemble each other. In fact, it is these very rivalries that lead them to adopt similar tactics and strategies even when they start with different social and economic objectives.

An institution is different from a mere collection of individuals. It has a life of its own and has not only its own aims and objectives but also its own interests which are different from those of its individual leaders including its supreme leader. It is true that powerful leaders are able to channel the activities of the party in ways that serve their personal interests even at the expense of those of the party. But it is always possible in the case of the party, at least in principle, to distinguish the interests of the institution from those of the individual. This is difficult, if not impossible, to do in the case of the faction which is only another way of saying that the faction, unlike the party, is not an institution.

In a comparative study of factions in different parts of the world, including India, Ralph Nicholas (1965: 28–9) pointed out, 'Members can be connected to a faction only through the activity of a leader since the unit has no corporate existence or clear single principle of recruitment.' He showed that the faction leader 'ordinarily has several different kinds of connections with his followers; he makes use of all possible ties to draw supporters into his faction' (Ibid.: 29). In other words, although the faction might act as a political association, it need not be constituted to act as a specifically political one.

Whereas political parties are limited in number even in a multiparty system, it is difficult, if not impossible, to tell the number of factions in any society at any point of time. It is difficult to count their number even in a limited geographical area because factions are by nature amorphous and fluid, running into each other, without the clear boundaries and the continuity over time characteristic of an institution such as the political party. They overlap each other, split apart, and combine with each other continuously over time.

Factions have been studied extensively by social anthropologists in rural India as a part of their interest in local-level politics. As they began to look more and more closely at the Indian village through field-studies that began in the wake of independence, they saw that while the divisions of caste and lineage were undoubtedly important, what mattered as much were the divisions of faction which cut across lineage and caste. It is faction, rather than caste, that drives the engine of local politics (Lewis 1958). Leaders of rival factions often belong to the same caste and even to the same lineage and their followers come from more than one caste or one lineage. In all cases, it is personal loyalty that counts, but such loyalty need not last very long, shifting from one person to another and, perhaps, back again. Factional divisions are from the sociological point of view different not only from the divisions of party, but also from those of caste. Whereas social anthropologists made considerable efforts to distinguish analytically between faction and caste, their counterparts among political scientists did not make the same kind of effort to distinguish between faction and party.

His studies of local politics in rural Orissa led British anthropologist F.G. Bailey (1969) to formulate and develop the concept of 'parapolitical systems' which are systems in which political actions and relations are not clearly differentiated from the social order in which they are embedded. Their political code gives priority to personal loyalty over commitment to impersonal rules. They operate more through networks of patronage than through the requirements of political or administrative office.

It has to be recognized that factional politics has its own code of conduct with its own obligations of loyalty and reciprocity. We will fail to appreciate the vitality and resilience of factions in our public life if we presume that they are driven solely by the pursuit of material advantage. They too have their code of obligation and loyalty although that code is not identical with what is appropriate to the working of political parties in a modern democracy.

Factions are not confined to rural communities. In India and elsewhere they permeate many if not most domains of social life. The interpenetration of factions and parties affects the relationship between government and opposition by making the boundaries of the party unclear and unstable. Nowhere is party politics fully insulated from factional politics, but the viability and strength of the party as an institution depends to some extent on that insulation.

An important study of the Congress party made less than two decades after independence revealed the part played by factions in the operation of the party. The study drew attention to the importance of personal relations in the operation of the political process as a whole. It said, 'Although the language of conflict is often phrased in terms of important principles and although a policy issue may sometimes be seized upon as a pretext for factional struggle, factions and factional conflicts are organized completely around personalities and around personal enmities among party leaders' (Brass 1965: 54). And further, 'Alliances develop and splits and defections occur wholly because of the mutual convenience and temporarily shared power-political interests of group leaders' (Ibid.).

Brass attempted a comparison between India and the United States in the now somewhat outdated framework of political development. He said:

> The essential difference politically between an Indian faction … and a faction in the American South lies in the primacy of factional interest over party loyalty in the former. In the American South, factional organization and conflict do not usually take precedence over party loyalty. Defeated factions in the South do not usually go into opposition, as very often happens in India. (Ibid.: 234)

The movement of factions from one party to another has increased vastly since Brass made his study, being both a cause and a consequence of the great increase in the number of political parties.

Defections from one party to another have reached such proportions in India that Parliament has had to enact legislation to penalize 'floor-crossing', or defection within the House. However, such legislation can do little to prevent the movement of persons from one party to another outside the legislature. The movement of individuals from one party to another takes place in all political systems including those in which parties rest on firm institutional foundations. Winston Churchill made himself notorious by moving, first, from the Conservative to the Liberal Party, and then back again from the Liberal to the Conservative Party, but such movement has become so common in India as to leave party leaders in a constant state of anxiety about which of their followers or allies can be trusted to remain loyal and faithful.

Coalition politics has given a new twist to the relationship between government and opposition. While there is a law which prevents defection from one party to another, a coalition partner is free to withdraw its support from one block and either remain neutral or transfer support to another block. Such transfers may have something to do with matters of policy or even principle, but they cannot be made effective without the offer of material inducements. It is difficult to estimate how much money does actually change hands in the movement of individuals from one party to another outside the House or of parties from one block to another within it, but the sums alleged in the media are enormous. Power brokers are constantly in negotiation with their allies, their rivals, and their opponents to keep the party or the block of parties together and, if possible, to augment its strength. The compulsions of coalition politics keep the balance between parties in a constant state of unstable equilibrium.

The uncertain and volatile nature of the relations between parties in a coalition, whether in government or opposition, creates an undercurrent of suspicion and mistrust, not only between adversaries recognized as such but also among individuals and groups expected to work towards a common purpose. The suspicion and mistrust do not go away when a partner does not actually withdraw support but only threatens to do so. They are magnified in the relations among parties that face each other as opposing blocks in Parliament.

* * *

The chronic mistrust between government and opposition impairs the foundations of democracy. Mistrust and suspicion on one side is met with concealment and evasion on the other. The very purpose of shaping the opposition into a responsible and legitimate political institution is frustrated.

Why have our political parties failed to find or sustain that fundamental basis of mutual trust without which the relations between government and opposition remain bitter, acrimonious, and wasteful? The reasons for the unsatisfactory state of the relations between government and opposition in our country lie partly in the social environment in which they operate. That environment, as I have tried to show, tends to give primacy to the faction over the party. But the historical conditions under which our parties have grown and developed have also played their part. Having devoted considerable space to the social environment in the earlier part of this essay and in previous essays, I would now like to turn to the distinctive historical conditions under which the party system originated and grew in this country.

The historical conditions were such as to give a pre-eminent, not to say a unique, place to one single party, namely, the Indian National Congress. As I have already noted, the Congress party is among the oldest political parties in the world. It is not only older than the Labour Party of the United Kingdom, but its foundation predates the foundation of the Communist parties of Russia and China. It has maintained its name and its claim to a certain political tradition for well over a hundred years. It made a successful transition from being a party of notables to being a party of the common people under the leadership of Mahatma Gandhi.

The Congress established its political position in the country through its consistent opposition to colonial rule and its leadership of the nationalist movement. It stood, from the very beginning, for the unity of India whereas its main adversary during the struggle for independence, the Muslim League, demanded the partition of India. Its opposition to the Muslim League during the struggle for independence was carried over into a mistrust of all political parties that had or appeared to have a special association with any religious group, such as the Hindu Mahasabha and its various later incarnations.

It is this historical association that makes it difficult for forward-looking Indians to feel at ease with any party that identifies itself with Hindutva. When they give it their support, they do so with an uneasy conscience, saying that the many misdeeds of the Congress party leave them with very little choice. The uneasy conscience of Indians with a liberal outlook over parties with a religious or sectarian association is in contrast with what is considered acceptable in European countries such as Germany which have had less difficulty in accommodating parties with a 'Christian' label. The difference between a 'Christian' party in Europe and a 'Hindu' party in India lies in the troubled history of the relationship between religion and nation-building in

India's recent past. The Congress has always stood for the unity of India as a single nation without consideration of religious difference, and it is this that enables it to claim the moral high ground over parties that smack of religious or sectarian bias.

The Congress leadership has sought to distance itself not only from sectarian parties but also from Communist parties, but for reasons of a different kind. Dr Ambedkar—no Congressman himself—had said in the Constituent Assembly, 'The Communist Party wants a Constitution based upon the principle of the Dictatorship of the Proletariat. They condemn the Constitution because it is based upon parliamentary democracy' (*CAD* 1989, XI: 975). The Communists have over the years shown some capacity to adapt themselves to the demands of multiparty rule, but the basic instinct of any Leninist party is to aspire towards single-party rule, and where they have been called upon to govern, they have tended to ignore the distinction between their party and the government formed by it.

An additional reason for the mistrust of the Communist Party among leaders of the nationalist movement was the feeling that it had loyalties outside the country and could not be trusted to put the interests of the nation first. These misgivings are not without historical foundation. At the time of independence, when Stalin was still alive, the leader who occupied the first place in the minds of the Communists was neither Jawaharlal Nehru nor Rajendra Prasad but the general secretary of the Communist Party of the Soviet Union. As many then said, the spiritual 'fatherland' of the Communists was not India but the USSR. Much has changed since that time, but the Communist leadership of the country has not done itself any service by its deferential attitude first towards the USSR and then towards the People's Republic of China.

It will not be an exaggeration to say that at the time of independence the great leaders of the nation were all leaders of the Congress party: Nehru, Patel, Azad, and many others, with Gandhi himself towering above the rest, although by then he had become aloof from the affairs of the party and had only a few months to live. No other political party had leaders with whose portraits the common people of the country were nearly as familiar. While most political parties now acknowledge Gandhi's heritage, the Congress believes that it has a special claim on that heritage because of its historical association with it.

It is important to appreciate the moral reasons on whose basis the Congress claims its unique position among the political parties in India, although those moral reasons are often used as a cover for the pursuit of naked material interests. The Congress leadership of today may admit that they have failed in many ways to live up to their great heritage; but to fall short of a great heritage is one thing, and to be without such a heritage is a different thing altogether.

After independence had been won and the country divided, and with the Muslim League out of the way, it seemed natural for the Congress leadership to feel that it had come into its own particular inheritance. Some had fought for the rights of the minorities, some for the rights of the backward communities, and some for the rights of workers and peasants, but the Congress party maintained that it alone had fought to bring freedom to the whole country. Nehru wanted to carry all Indians along with him. In forming his first cabinet he included persons from outside the Congress, including some who had been staunch opponents of it, such as B.R. Ambedkar and Shyama Prasad Mookerjee.

Not everybody in his party had Nehru's spirit of accommodation. Others in it viewed the leaders of opposition parties with condescension and contempt. As the Congress party became weaker and less self-assured with the passage of time, to contempt and condescension was added an element of fear. Nehru's daughter, being suspicious rather than trustful by nature, had a shrewd judgement of all her opponents, including those within her own party. As the number of claimants for perquisites and patronage grew within the party itself, there was very little scope for treating opponents with any degree of generosity.

The deficit of trust between the Congress and the other parties did not decline after Indira Gandhi's two terms of office, but increased. Its brief spells in opposition did little to moderate the view the party held of its opponents. While in office, its members began to act and speak as if they alone had the right to rule, not just during their allotted term of office but for all time. This has done little to encourage responsible conduct among members of the opposition. When they are unable to make their voices heard in Parliament, they disturb its proceedings and take to the streets in an effort to paralyse the government.

The Emergency of 1975–7 brought relations between government and opposition close to the breaking point. It shook people's faith in the government, but what followed the Emergency did little to enhance their faith in the opposition. Since the Emergency, the government, of no matter which party or coalition of parties, has shown its feet of clay to the opposition over and over again. A large part of the opposition's time and energy is spent in catching the government on the wrong foot. An almost equally large part of the government's time and energy is spent in prevarication and evasive action. In this process both government and opposition lose their focus and, ultimately, their legitimacy. It becomes a hard task to sustain the spirit of democracy when the very institutions designed to embody that spirit have to contend with mistrust and suspicion at every step.

At the time of independence the Congress party took upon itself the historical responsibility of building democracy in India (Guha 2007). It was then the only party that could be reasonably expected to undertake such a responsibility. It had inherited a great political tradition and it enjoyed abundant popular support. Its success in this endeavour has been at best limited.

There are many reasons behind the limited success of the Congress party. When in office, its leaders become so accustomed to its comforts that they find it painful to make room for others even within their own party, and show remarkable tenacity in holding on to their perquisites. Corruption has become a minor industry in the Congress party, and in that it has set an example for other parties. The party's bondage to its first family has also set a bad example for others.

Beyond that there is a failure of imagination that weakens the fabric of democracy. A major political party has the right to believe that it can govern the country better than any other party. But that is different from believing that no other party can be trusted to govern the country if it carries a different name or has a different history and a different political outlook. As that belief insinuates itself into the Congress consciousness, it begins to distort the very operation of democracy which requires the alternation of parties in the larger interest of the nation. If the leaders of the party are so possessive about their hold over the nation as to deny to any other party the moral right to govern it, then they must ask themselves what democracy means to them.

References

Bailey, F.G. 1969. *Stratagems and Spoils*. Oxford: Basil Blackwell.

Béteille, André. 1980. 'The Indian Village: Past and Present', in E.J. Hobsbawm, Witold Kula, Ashok Mitra, K.N. Raj, and Ignacy Sachs (eds), *Peasants in History*, Calcutta: Oxford University Press, pp. 107–20.

———. 2000. 'Anarchy and Abuse of Power', *Economic and Political Weekly*, vol. xxxv, no. 10, pp. 779–83.

Blair, Tony. 2010. *A Journey*. London: Hutchinson.

Brass, Paul R. 1965. *Factional Politics in an Indian State*. Berkeley: University of California Press.

Bullock, Alan. 1993. *Hitler and Stalin*. New York: Vintage Books.

Campbell, Alistair. 2007. *The Alistair Campbell Diaries: The Blair Years*. New York: Alfred Knopf.

Constituent Assembly Debates (CAD). 1989. *Official Report*. New Delhi: Government of India, vols VII and XI.

Dandavate, Madhu. 1996. 'Role and Position of the Leader of the Opposition', in D. Sundar Rau (ed.), *Readings in Indian Parliamentary Opposition*, New Delhi: Kanishka Publishers, pp. 59–68.

Dhar, P.N. 2000. *Indira Gandhi, the 'Emergency' and Indian Democracy*. New Delhi: Oxford University Press.

Duverger, Maurice. 1954. *Political Parties*. London: Methuen.

Figes, Orlando. 2007. *The Whisperers*. London: Allen Lane.

Gandhi, M.K. 1962. *Village Swaraj*. Ahmedabad: Navajivan Publishing House.

Guha, Ramachandra. 2007. *India After Gandhi*. London: Macmillan.

Hsu, Francis L.K. 1963. *Clan, Caste and Club*. Princeton: Van Nostrand.

Lewis, Oscar. 1958. *Village Life in North India*. Urbana: University of Illinois Press.

Narayan, Jayaprakash. 1959. *A Plea for Reconstruction of Indian Polity*. Varanasi: Sarva Seva Sangh Prakashan.

————. 1978. *Total Revolution*. Bombay: Popular Prakashan.

Nicholas, Ralph W. 1965. 'Factions: A Comparative Analysis', in Michael Banton (ed.), *Political Systems and the Distribution of Power*, London: Tavistock, pp. 21–61.

Norton, Philip. 1981. *The Commons in Perspective*. Oxford: Martin Robertson.

Pipes, Richard. 1991. *The Russian Revolution*. New York: Vintage Books.

Scott, James C. 1985. *Weapons of the Weak*. New Haven: Yale University Press.

3

Civil Society and the State

This chapter is devoted to a discussion of civil society and the state with special emphasis on the former. Civil society is viewed here as a set of institutions that embody the social side, as it were, of democracy whose political side is represented by the legislature, the judiciary, and the other institutions discussed in Chapter 1. The relationship between state and civil society is a complex one. In a constitutional democracy they are, at least in principle, complementary. They cannot be viewed as substitutes for each other, or as dedicated adversaries. Each has its own contribution to make to the well-being of the nation.

When I speak of civil society as a set of institutions, I have in mind the enduring character of those institutions which marks them out from voluntary associations, many of which are too short-lived to pass muster as institutions. I also regard them as distinct from social movements which cannot be reckoned as institutions because of their lack of shape and form. No doubt a voluntary association or a social movement may acquire the character of an institution if in course of time it acquires a distinct and enduring identity.

The state has been regarded as one of the pre-eminent institutions of society. It is, in effect, a complex of institutions having distinct forms and functions rather than a single, unitary institution. There are differences of opinion among legal and political theorists on the specific organs that may or may not be included in its definition. The state derives its significance from the fact that it is viewed as the ultimate source of legitimate authority, although coercion, domination, and manipulation often operate at the margins of the state and in the interstices between it and the other institutions of society.

The state figures more prominently in the writings of legal and political theorists than in those of sociologists and social anthropologists. When sociologists study the state, they do so most often in relation to the other institutions of society. Compared to the state, which has received scholarly attention since ancient and medieval times, civil society has attracted attention only in modern times. The idea of civil society, first developed in the West in the eighteenth and nineteenth centuries, acquired a new lease of life in the closing decades of the twentieth century. Partly because political scientists have played a leading role in the revival of interest in civil society, it has come to be discussed very widely in relation to the state. Even where the sociologist is concerned primarily with civil society, he cannot discuss it fruitfully in isolation from the state.

Sociologists recognize that, despite its great contemporary and historical importance, the state as an institution has not existed everywhere or at all times. More than seventy years ago, social anthropologists drew attention to the distinction between societies with states and stateless societies (Fortes and Evans-Pritchard 1940). In the early stages of evolution, stateless societies were the norm and many examples of them could still be found as relatively autonomous systems into the early part of the twentieth century. But the expansion of the state that began with imperial rule in the eighteenth and nineteenth centuries has in every part of the world whittled down their autonomy, and most populations have now come under the embrace of one state or another.

The relationship between state and civil society has been a subject of debate and discussion since the early part of the nineteenth century. Hegel took a somewhat idealized view of the state and his conception of civil society was formal and abstract rather than concrete or empirical. He situated his observations on civil society within his scheme of the succession of historical epochs in which it constituted a phase or, in his phrase, a 'moment' between the family on the one hand and the state on the other. This succession is governed by a two-fold dialectic, of altruism and egoism on the one hand, and of the particular and the universal on the other. In Hegel's scheme, civil society expresses the moment of universal egoism following upon that of the particular altruism of the family and to be succeeded by that of the universal altruism of the state.

The state that Hegel visualized as the embodiment of universal altruism failed to materialize. When, on the other hand, we look at the actual forms taken by the state in the last 200 years, we are struck by their great, not to say inexhaustible, variety. A casual glance at the list of the states that are constituents of the United Nations will give some idea of their variety in the present world. Even that would hardly cover the entire range of the states that have risen and fallen in the course of human history: tribal states, imperial states, feudal monarchies, constitutional monarchies, bourgeois democracies, peoples' democracies, and totalitarian states.

Among the many different types of state known to students of society and history, the constitutional state based on the impersonal rule of law occupies a special place in contemporary discussions of state and civil society. A written constitution which both sets forth and limits the powers of the state and contains clear procedures for its own revision is a distinctive feature of the modern world. Its operation depends upon the presence of specific social and cultural conditions that are themselves modern rather than medieval or ancient. It is often said that a modern constitution is bound to be ineffectual or even dysfunctional when it is artificially planted on an uncongenial soil (Chapter 4 in this volume). This anxiety is at the heart of the present discussion of state and society in many parts of the world.

The compatibility between state and society is a vexed, not to say an intractable, question. No satisfactory test of it exists, and it is difficult to see how a workable test can be devised. For one thing, while it may be possible to define the state, or at least the constitutional state, the position is somewhat different when we take society as a whole and particularly a society in transition. A society is a field of conflicting forces which accommodates not only disparate forms of organization but also divergent norms and values.

The creation of the modern state has in many parts of the world entailed a rupture with past ways of life and thought. The French Revolution created such a rupture at the end of the eighteenth century and the Bolshevik Revolution at the beginning of the twentieth century. Old structures of authority were dismantled and new ones put in their place; old laws were replaced by new ones. But we know with the advantage of hindsight that changes in the formal structures of authority embodied in the state did not bring about corresponding changes across society as a whole. Old social arrangements were often transformed, but not always in conformity with the designs of the new structures of authority.

A large number of new states came into existence with the end of colonial rule in the middle of the twentieth century. The creation of new states has not come to an end as the experiences of central and eastern Europe at the end of the twentieth century would show. There are two lessons to be learnt from these experiences across the world. First, creating a new society is very different from creating a new state. Second, habits and practices that are deeply rooted in society act back on the new structures of authority and subvert the rules prescribed for their operation.

*   *   *

The concept of civil society has had more than one incarnation. Although it appears in the philosophical writings of seventeenth-century authors such as Hobbes and Locke, it may be said to have entered the social sciences in the second half of the eighteenth century with the work of the Scottish moral philosophers. A typical example of this work is Adam Ferguson's *An Essay on the History of Civil Society* (1966), first published in 1767. Here there is a clear shift of focus from the state to society, and the approach adopted is a comparative one.

Ferguson's starting point was the distinction between 'civil society' and 'natural society'. For him civil society was not only the site for the pursuit of private interest, it was also the site for the practice of civility. He believed that there was a secular tendency, at least in the European countries, towards a movement from natural to civil society. Civil society drew man out of his natural condition in which unrestrained passions held sway, and it encouraged the orderly pursuit of private interests through the practice of civility (Hirschman 1977). Ferguson himself was both a member of a Scottish clan and a leader of the movement known as the Scottish Enlightenment. As such, he viewed with some ambivalence the displacement of a society based on kinship, clan, and community by one based on a rational division of labour.

Later authors within the same tradition pointed out that civil society was accompanied not only by the pursuit of individual interest but also by the development of a new type of associational life. Most notable among these was the nineteenth-century French writer Alexis de Tocqueville (1956). His approach too was empirical and comparative. He had travelled to the United States where he observed at first hand the profuse growth of associations. The associations he observed had been created by conscious human effort, and as such were quite different from the traditional (or 'natural') groupings of kinship, clanship, and caste that had existed in Europe and other countries since time immemorial.

The expansion of new forms of associational life and their implications for social order and stability became an important preoccupation with European sociologists in the second half of the nineteenth century. Toennies's contrast between Gemeinschaft and Gesellschaft, or community and association, first formulated in 1887, became a byword among sociologists (Toennies 1957). Many felt that the decline of the community and its replacement by the association, no matter what its economic benefits, would weaken the fabric of social life. Durkheim (1984) took a contrary view and argued that societies based on the division of labour would be more cohesive than those based on communities of birth, provided strong associations based on occupation were encouraged to grow in them.

Responding to the potential for disorder caused by rapid economic change, Durkheim argued strongly for the creation and strengthening of professional associations. For him, the professional association was indispensable 'not because of the services it might render, but on account of the moral influence it could exercise' (Durkheim 1984: xxxiv). He went on to argue, 'A nation cannot be maintained unless, between the state and individuals, a whole range of secondary groups are interposed. These must be close enough to the individual to attract him strongly to their activities and, in so doing, to absorb him into the mainstream of social life' (Ibid.: liv). Durkheim saw very clearly that modern professional associations could not be like the medieval guilds but had to be open and secular institutions.

The term used by both Hegel and Marx for what we are now discussing was 'Bürgerlichegesellschaft' which may be translated into English as either 'civil society' or 'bourgeois society'. For Marx and his followers it was linked with the ascendancy of a particular social class for which the term 'bourgeoisie' came to be widely used. Both Hegel and Marx adopted an ambivalent attitude towards civil society or bourgeois society. They did not regard it as either the end point of history or the highest form of historical development but at best as a necessary stage in the development of the good society.

When Adam Ferguson wrote of civil society or Hegel of Bürgerlichegesellschaft, they had in mind mainly European or western society. Alexis de Tocqueville drew attention to the great significance of American society in this context, but that too was a branch of western society. Even for Marx, who believed that capitalist domination would spread throughout the world, the locus of bourgeois society lay essentially in the West. The countries of Africa, Asia, and Latin America were far from the thoughts of nineteenth-century western scholars when they reflected on the nature and significance of civil society.

The problem that students of society and politics face today is to determine whether and in what form the idea of civil society can be extended to the countries of Asia, Africa, and Latin America whose social formations are very different from those of the West. The idea of civil society has since the last few decades been given a new lease of life by the prospects of its application to a whole range of new

societies including those of eastern and central Europe (Hahn 1990).
While some write freely of civil society, or civil society institutions in
what used to be called the 'developing areas', others wonder how far
the idea of civil society can be stretched without being made to lose
its core or essential meaning. Indeed, the core or essential meaning
of civil society has itself now come under question (Hahn and Dunn
1996; Elliott 2003).

The recent growth of interest in civil society across the globe is the
outcome of a number of different factors. A great deal was expected
of the state in the new nations that emerged in the wake of World
War II and decolonization. The state has failed, and sometimes failed
very badly to deliver what was expected from it. It has been either
oppressive or ineffectual, and often both. Instead of contributing to
democracy and development it has become a burden on the people.
A great deal of the enthusiasm for civil society has been born from
the disenchantment with the state and the search for an alternative
motive force for democracy and development. Today many have
come to the point where they think of the state as the oppressor
and civil society as the redeemer. Is it reasonable to think of the
relationship between state and civil society in this way?

The current interest in civil society is not confined to social
scientists or even to intellectuals in general. Political leaders,
including heads of state and government, social activists, and public
intellectuals all point to its value and importance. An interesting
recent development is the promotion of the idea of civil society by
a variety of international agencies. In particular those agencies that
support development work in the countries of Asia, Africa, and Latin
America, seek the involvement of civil society in such work. Similar
concerns began to emerge in the countries of eastern and central
Europe with the break-up of the Soviet system.

A positive connotation has thus come to be attached to the
idea of civil society, particularly where it comes to developing or
transitional societies. This is not in conformity with the original
usage, particularly in the German language. Neither Hegel nor Marx
regarded civil society as the equivalent of the good society. They
both used the term 'Bürgerlichegesellschaft' which in course of time

came to acquire a negative connotation. With the new vogue for civil society that emerged in the last two decades of the twentieth century, a new term 'Zivilgesellschaft' has come into use. It is a neologism based on a direct adaptation of the English phrase. The new coinage is a belated acknowledgement by German writers of the need to distinguish between bourgeois society and civil society, and it conveys much better the positive connotation that its users would like to give to the idea.

* * *

Despite the current popularity of the term in different parts of the world, civil society is a historical category and not a universal category of human existence. Whether as a type or an aspect of society, it does not exist everywhere nor has it existed at all times. Its existence depends upon the presence of particular economic, political, and cultural conditions. We cannot speak meaningfully of civil society in the absence of a certain legal framework and its operation in prescribed ways. To undertake a social movement, no matter how far-reaching, for the creation of civil society, is not the same thing as having it. Civil society is not just a social movement, it is also a set of institutions.

One cannot expect to find civil society among populations that are organized on a tribal basis, or on the basis mainly of clan and caste. Adam Ferguson saw quite clearly the distinction between the clan-based social order that had come down from the past in his native Scotland and the new one emerging in the wake of changes in the legal and economic framework. It was only the latter and not the former that corresponded to his conception of civil society. It is not that clan-based or caste-based societies lack law and morality, but their legal and moral presuppositions are of a different kind.

Civil society as a distinctive set of institutions emerged in a particular part of the world during a particular phase of history. It is not possible to specify in exact terms the place or the time of its emergence, but western Europe in the eighteenth and nineteenth centuries may be taken as the ground on which the seeds of civil society began to germinate. In western Europe civil society was not the product of any deliberate or concerted effort to bring it into being. It was rather the unintended consequence of many changes in the material conditions and the ideological climate of society. This of course does not mean that it cannot be brought into existence by conscious political effort elsewhere and under other conditions.

Civil society as a distinctive set of ideas, institutions, and social arrangements is a feature of the modern world. The ideas, institutions, and arrangements that give it a distinctive character did not exist or existed only fitfully and sporadically in the medieval or ancient world. But the fact that it is a distinctive feature of the modern world does not mean that it exists everywhere in it or is developed to the same extent or in the same form in every country. Civil society in France does not have the same character as civil society in the United States. This was already noted by Alexis de Tocqueville in the first half of the nineteenth century. At the same time, they must show a certain family resemblance for both to be described by the same phrase.

The experience of the twentieth century shows not only that civil society emerges only under certain historical conditions but also that its continued existence cannot be taken for granted. The suppression of civil society in Germany during the decade or so of Hitler's rule is a favourite example. It is true that in comparison with Britain and France, Germany was a relative latecomer to modernity, but the institutions of civil society, including the legal framework required for their sustenance and growth, were clearly in place by the beginning of the twentieth century. The entire legal and institutional framework was disrupted within a few years and civil society set back in its course by the rise of the Nazi state. But it must be remembered that the interregnum, no matter how traumatic, lasted for barely a dozen years, and civil society was restored to its place, at least in the Federal Republic of Germany, within a few years of the establishment of the new post-war regime.

The case of Russia in the twentieth century is both more complex and more interesting. It raises questions about the conditions not only for the emergence of civil society but also for its supersession.

For while it is undoubtedly true that under Stalin state and party made short work of the rule of law, the rights of citizens, and the autonomy of institutions, it is also true that these features of civil society were neither very strong nor very secure in the Tsarist regime that existed prior to the Bolshevik Revolution. It may well be that Communism succeeded in snuffing out social arrangements whose foundations were infirm to begin with.

I have said that the relationship between civil society and the state should not be viewed as a relationship between adversaries. At the same time, the institutions that give shape and form to civil society have to be distinct and autonomous from the state. Where they have failed to safeguard their autonomy, civil society has withered.

With the break-up of the Soviet system a new interest in the building of civil society began to emerge in the countries of eastern and central Europe. These countries had entered the socialist system with very diverse historical backgrounds, and their experience of socialist control was not as prolonged as in the Soviet Union. Some of them, such as the German Democratic Republic, Czechoslovakia, and Hungary, had developed legal institutions and economic systems more in tune with the requirements of civil society than those prevalent in most parts of Russia whereas others, such as Bulgaria and Romania, were still on the threshold of modernity.

When these countries became free from the yoke of Communist rule, their new leaders attributed the weakness of civil society to the tyranny of the socialist system. One of the most prominent of such leaders, Vaclav Havel (1993) wrote about the destructive effects of socialist rule on the institutions of society. But liberation from the socialist state did not automatically bring back into being the kind of society it is alleged to have suppressed. In these circumstances there are, as one would expect, disagreements over what civil society actually means and whether it can be expected to have the same content in eastern as in western Europe (Hahn and Dunn 1996).

The present worldwide concern for civil society has led public intellectuals and makers of opinion in many countries in Asia and Africa to look for the roots of civil society in their own pre-colonial past.

There is no doubt that colonial rule created states that were oppressive and unjust, and discriminated against the native population. It also dismantled or undermined many established social arrangements. But from that it may not be reasonable to conclude that colonial rule put an end to civil society in India or Indonesia or Nigeria, when it hardly had a place in the social traditions of those countries in pre-colonial times.

Civil society grows along with new ideas, new values, and new forms of institutional and associational life. These have now acquired a certain universal appeal, particularly among the politically conscious intelligentsia, but their growth has been very uneven in the different countries of the world, and, within the same country, among the different classes and strata. To be sure, the growth may be obstructed by an oppressive state, colonial or ex-colonial, totalitarian or ex-totalitarian. But it may be thwarted also by pervasive and deep-rooted social traditions whose principles of operation are not in tune with those by which civil society is governed.

*   *   *

The historical process that has led to the emergence of civil society in the different parts of the world may be understood in the framework of three specific phenomena. These are (i) the constitutional state, (ii) universal citizenship, and (iii) open and secular institutions that mediate between the first and the second. These three phenomena are homologous and interrelated. Together they constitute a set that is distinctive of the modern world, though by no means universally present or equally developed in all contemporary societies.

To repeat what has already been noted, state and civil society are complementary and not antagonistic. In Hegel's scheme the state was assigned not only a positive value, but a higher value than civil society. Though neither Marx nor his successor and follower Antonio Gramsci assigned a very high value to civil society, they viewed the state as being basically an engine of oppression. This view of the state has acquired wide currency among social activists and public intellectuals in many countries, particularly in Asia, Africa, and Latin America. The valuation of state and civil society that characterized Hegel's approach has in some sense been reversed.

When I speak of the state as being complementary to civil society, I have in mind not every kind of state but, specifically, the modern constitutional state based on the impersonal rule of law. The constitutional state based on the rule of law is an innovation, and a fairly recent innovation in most parts of the world. Anxiety about the malfunctioning of the state is one thing; looking for an alternative to it in civil society is another. To maintain that state and civil society are complementary is to imply that a division of functions exists between them. This division cannot be fixed once and for all, but just as the state cannot appropriate all the functions of civil society, so too civil society cannot act in the place of the state in every sphere.

A constitution not only lays down the powers of the state, it also lays down the limits to those powers. The self-limitation of its own powers in accordance with prescribed rules and procedures is a distinctive feature of the constitutional state. Civil society grows in those spaces in which the state does not ordinarily impose its powers. If the state did not allow the growth of autonomous institutions outside its direct control, civil society would not be possible. This does not mean that the state must completely renounce its authority over such institutions, but the exercise of that authority has to be regulated by law and convention.

Constitutionalism is not a universal value. Even in the contemporary world it does not have the same meaning and force in all societies everywhere. Where its roots are shallow, its rules and procedures appear cumbersome, obstructive, and even unjust, and are easily set aside in response to social and political pressures. The repeated violation of those rules and procedures undermines the legitimacy of the constitutional state and makes it appear at the same time both oppressive and impotent. The constitutional state cannot work effectively where constitutional values are lightly treated.

The making of the Constitution of India was a watershed in the country's political and social life. Dr Ambedkar, who piloted it through the Constituent Assembly, drew pointed attention to the fragility of what he called 'constitutional morality' (Chapter 4 in this volume). The basis of constitutional morality is a respect for formally prescribed rules and procedures equally by the functionaries of the state and its citizens. A modern constitution is a man-made document written in such a manner as to make its rules and procedures consistent with each other to the maximum extent possible. The Constitution of India has been criticized for being too lengthy and too detailed. Dr Ambedkar argued that even the details of administration had to be written into it because constitutional morality was infirm in India. Where it was well established, those details could be left in the hands of subordinate agencies.

While Dr Ambedkar dealt specifically with the Indian case, his observations on constitutional morality have a very wide application. State formation in most of the newly independent countries of Asia and Africa has been bedevilled by one kind of constitutional crisis or another. India was in some sense an exception in being able to complete the work of creating a coherent constitution as a framework of a new kind of state. Pakistan's limited success with creating an acceptable constitution, despite successive attempts, is an indication of the infirmity of both constitutional morality and civil society in that country.

The experience of Russia in the twentieth century throws light from another angle on the precarious foundations of the constitutional state. The Tsarist state cannot be properly called a constitutional state although constitutional values were beginning to emerge under its shadow. The Bolshevik Revolution aimed not so much to create constitutional values as to establish the dictatorship of the proletariat. As the Soviet system became entrenched under Stalin and his successors, it undermined the rule of law on which the constitutional state is based and at the same time gave short shrift to the rights of citizenship.

The development of universal citizenship is intimately linked with the development of the constitutional state. Civil society is first and foremost a society of citizens; without the rights and obligations of citizenship there is no civil society. This is most clearly seen when a despotic or totalitarian state sets at nought the rights of citizens.

But citizenship is not a matter merely of legal or even political rights; it is, above all, a social value based on respect for the individual as an autonomous moral agent.

Not all societies are societies of citizens. Many societies are or have been societies of castes and communities, or of clans and lineages. The modern concept of citizenship is that it is a direct relationship between the individual and the state mediated only by institutions that are compatible with constitutional values. The entitlements of citizenship are not dependent on the individual's membership of a lineage, a clan, or a caste. In many parts of the world citizenship is a new idea and a new value. Meyer Fortes (1970: 147), who studied the kingdom of Ashanti in West Africa, tells us that 'it is a fundamental principle of Ashanti law that lineage membership is an inextinguishable jural capacity and the basic credential for citizenship'. It was somewhat similar in traditional Hindu society where the individual was a member of society by virtue of his membership of a caste, and where, until the Removal of Caste Disabilities Act was passed in 1850, expulsion from caste amounted to civil death.

While it is true that the British in India, like the Dutch in Indonesia or the French in Algeria, denied the substance of citizenship to their colonial subjects, it is also true that they implanted the idea of citizenship in the minds of increasing numbers of those same subjects. The idea grew and acquired substance in and through the movement for emancipation from colonial rule. Naturally, citizenship did not acquire the same form or substance in all the countries after they attained independence. The form and substance acquired by it depended on the initial conditions in the country in question and also on the course taken by the movement for freedom. It would be a mistake to regard citizenship in countries like India as a gift of colonial rule; but it would be a mistake also to deny to that rule a catalytic role in its development (Chapter 6 in this volume). In the end, it matters less where a social ideal comes from than what people make of it.

Although the idea of citizenship had acquired a wide appeal in western countries such as France and America by the end of the eighteenth century, the legal, political, and social components of citizenship grew slowly and unevenly. Citizenship did not become a fully inclusive condition all at once. Even in the narrowly legal sense, large sections of the population were denied the full benefits of citizenship on grounds of race, religion, and gender. It took a long time for women to acquire, as citizens, the same legal and political rights as men, and Blacks the same rights as Whites.

The enlargement of citizenship may be understood in more than one sense. First, hitherto excluded sections of society are granted citizenship which in that sense becomes more inclusive. In a purely formal sense the extension of the franchise provides a good example of this. If we look at the history of western democracies in the last 200 years, we will find that initially the franchise was restricted by property, by gender, and by race. Citizens consisted at first of a small and limited section of society, and it was that section that constituted the political public. As the franchise became extended in the twentieth century, citizenship became enlarged and the political public more inclusive.

Civil society is a set of institutions that mediate between the individual as a citizen and the state or nation. I will now describe very briefly what I mean by an institution and then try to identify the defining features of those institutions that constitute the bedrock, as it were, on which civil society rests (Béteille 2000: 172–97). An institution is an enduring group with definite boundaries and a distinct identity that outlives those who are its individual members at any point of time. The school from which I matriculated and which celebrated its centenary a few years ago is an institution. Libraries and hospitals are institutions. The Reserve Bank of India is an institution, and *The Times of India* is an institution.

Not all institutions contribute positively to the life of civil society as I understand it. Only open and secular institutions do so, and I have chosen my examples in the last paragraph from them. They are open in the sense that membership in them is independent of such considerations as race, caste, creed, and gender, and they are secular in the sense that their internal arrangements are not regulated by religious rules or religious authorities. It will be seen that the mediating institutions that I have singled out are homologous with the constitutional state and the individual as a citizen.

The constitutional state allows and even encourages the development of open and secular institutions, and their differentiation from itself and from each other. This means not only that the domains of finance, education, research, communications, and so on, become differentiated from each other, but that within each domain institutions of several kinds emerge, and often, several of each kind. The institutions of politics and administration become differentiated from each other, and a plurality of political parties and associations come into being. Civil society is characterized by the continuous differentiation of institutions and associations. Differentiation does not mean disconnection, the differentiated parts of civil society being interconnected through networks of various kinds. Civil society makes it possible for individuals as citizens to circulate between institutions and associations with far greater freedom than in societies based on kinship, caste, and community.

In civil society the plurality of institutions goes hand-in-hand with the autonomy of institutions. Respect for autonomy, whether of individuals or of institutions, is, again, not a 'natural sentiment'. It is the product of particular social and historical conditions. A state that does not respect the autonomy of institutions is unlikely to respect the rights of its citizens. But, again, the threat to the autonomy of institutions as well as of individuals may come not from the state alone but from emancipationist and antinomian social currents and movements even where such movements are described by their leaders and the media as 'civil society movements'.

Like voluntary associations, social movements have an important place in the life of a democracy, although they are so very diverse that their contribution can be evaluated only selectively. They may serve to strengthen civil society, but they may also be used to disrupt its institutions. It will be safe to say that movements that are directed against the government are the ones likely to receive the widest public attention. Many of the leaders of such movements have mastered the art of using television to further their cause. A kind of symbiotic relationship between such movements and the electronic media has now become an important part of public life in India.

Not all social movements are secular in their aims and objectives. Many of them are tacitly or even avowedly devoted to the promotion of sectarian interests. It is not always easy to detect or expose the sectarian bias in such movements because their leaders generally, if not invariably, say that they are challenging the authority of the state in the cause of social justice. In India nothing is more common than for members of a caste or a community to feel that they have been the victims of discrimination, oppression, and injustice. It is not easy in these circumstances to draw a clear line of distinction between what secular intellectuals and the media call 'civil society movements' and movements that demand redress from the state for real or alleged discrimination on grounds of caste and community.

The organization of social movements differs in terms of scale, atmosphere, and public attention. Some movements are organized on a modest scale, and their organizers are mindful of the requirements of public order. Others seek to attract maximum public attention and their organizers are not above disrupting public order to achieve their objective. Confrontation with the guardians of law and order leads to violence on both sides, and the television cameras are always in attendance to present 'breaking news' across the country.

Most social movements are transitory phenomena. They appear on the scene and then die out, to be replaced by others which go through more or less the same cycle of development. Some have a longer life span and continue, with ups and downs, for months if not years. The social movement to put pressure on the government to reclassify the Gujjar community as a Scheduled Tribe has continued for a long time, with repeated dislocations of road and rail traffic. The cumulative effect of such movements is to demoralize the functionaries of the state and to force them to act beyond their brief, either out of spite or from panic.

India's tradition of satyagraha has been an example to the whole world, and nobody can question the value of civil disobedience as a legitimate form of resistance to the oppression of the state. But civil disobedience has undergone a sea change between Mahatma Gandhi's time and ours. Gandhi maintained that the civil disobedient must submit his own conduct to stricter standards of moral scrutiny than the ordinary citizen. Today there are simply too many civil disobedients with too many personal and political ambitions for that to be seriously considered, let alone observed.

There has been a displacement of the moral core of civil disobedience by a political one. Gandhi used civil disobedience as a method of persuasion and not coercion. He agonized continuously over a legitimate method of resistance that might begin with the intention to persuade but take a turn towards coercion or even violence.

It is not at all my argument that the leaders of social movements today are devoid of probity, integrity, and sincerity. My concern is not so much with the intentions of the persons who initiate such movements as with their consequences. It has to be emphasized that while civil disobedience still remains a legitimate form of resistance, its present context is very different from its past context. One could argue that it was both politically and morally right to use civil disobedience to shake the colonial state to its very foundations. Can one make the same case for shaking the sovereign republic of independent India to its foundations?

Social movements in the cause of civil society and in opposition to the state and its functionaries are attracting increasing numbers of educated and talented persons with experience of professional life. They include lawyers, journalists, academics, and also retired judges, civil servants, and police officers. They are creating a new kind of quasi-political leadership which wants to exercise influence and power, but does not wish to be involved in politics or with political parties, whether of the government or the opposition, which they regard as venal, corrupt, and indifferent to the real needs and interests of the people.

This disenchantment extends from political parties to the electoral process. Politicians of the garden variety regard elections as the lifeblood of politics in a democracy. It is true that those same politicians have debased and corrupted the very process by which they swear. But if in addition to both government and opposition we also devalue and further undermine the electoral process, it is difficult to see what will remain of the institutions of democracy and of democracy itself.

References

Béteille, André. 2000. *Antinomies of Society.* New Delhi: Oxford University Press.

Durkheim, Émile. 1984. *The Division of Labour in Society.* New York: The Free Press.

Elliott, Carolyn M. (ed.). 2003. *Civil Society and Democracy.* New Delhi: Oxford University Press.

Ferguson, Adam. 1966. *An Essay on the History of Civil Society.* Edinburgh: Edinburgh University Press.

Fortes, Meyer. 1970. *Kinship and the Social Order: The Legacy of Lewis Henry Morgan.* London: Routledge and Kegal Paul.

Fortes, M. and E.E. Evans-Pritchard (eds). 1940. *African Political Systems.* London: Oxford University Press.

Hahn, Chris (ed.). 1990. *Market Economy and Civil Society in Hungary.* London: Frank Cass.

Hahn, Chris and Elizabeth Dunn (eds). 1996. *Civil Society.* London: Routledge.

Havel, Vaclav. 1993. 'The Post-Communist Nightmare', *New York Review of Books,* vol. xl, no. 10, 27 May.

Hirschman, Albert O. 1977. *The Passions and the Interests.* Princeton: Princeton University Press.

Tocqueville, Alexis de. 1956. *Democracy in America.* New York: Alfred Knopf, 2 vols.

Toennies, Ferdinand. 1957. *Community and Association.* London: Routledge and Kegan Paul.

4

Constitutional Morality*

Nearly thirty years ago when I gave the Ambedkar lectures at the University of Bombay, I chose as my subject the changing place of the backward classes in Indian society (Béteille 1981). That seemed a natural choice in view of my own interest in equality and inequality, and in view of Dr Ambedkar's towering position as a leader of the backward classes. Many developments in our social and political life have taken place since then, and I have developed my own ideas on the backward classes, on social exclusion, and on policies of affirmative action (Béteille 1987, 2002). I have decided not to go over the same ground again, but to speak on a different and, for me, a relatively new subject.

I have chosen to speak today on constitutional morality. Apart from its own intrinsic importance, it is a subject on which Dr Ambedkar spoke with insight and eloquence in the Constituent Assembly. It has been said that Dr Ambedkar has become an icon of the backward classes. This is certainly true. But he is also one of the makers of modern India and the architect of its present constitutional order. His observations on constitutional morality, made at a critical juncture in our social and political life, are of the utmost significance not only for the backward classes or the minorities, but for all Indians.

* This chapter was previously published in *Economic and Political Weekly*, vol. 43, no. 40, 2008, pp. 35–42.

The Constituent Assembly met in an atmosphere of great expectation. The country had attained freedom after a long period of colonial rule, and the possibilities of constructing a new social order based on liberty, equality, and social harmony seemed inexhaustible. From being subjects of an alien power Indians had become citizens in their own land. The Constituent Assembly brought together a galaxy of outstanding persons, remarkable for their intellectual ability, their political acumen, and their moral standing. Yet among all these persons Dr Ambedkar stood out as the most clear-sighted in his understanding of the contradictions facing Indian society at that time.

He saw more clearly than the others the pervasive contradictions between the hierarchical social structure inherited from the past and the urge for a democratic legal and political order forcefully expressed in the Assembly. Like the other members of it, he too had expectations about the future, but unlike most of them he had few illusions about the past. He did not believe that India had a democratic tradition in any meaningful sense; if such a tradition ever existed, it was in a distant past, long since lost in the mists of time. The social order of caste was antithetical to the political institutions of democracy, and caste had been the defining feature of Indian society since time immemorial.

No doubt the members of the Constituent Assembly were aware of the inequality, conflict, and disorder prevalent in Indian society in their time. But most of them had by then acquired the convenient habit of attributing every Indian misfortune to the misdeeds of colonial rule. That habit continues among large sections of the Indian intelligentsia to this day. If it is not colonialism, then it is neo-colonialism that is the villain. It does not speak well of us to shift the burden of responsibility for all our contradictions and dilemmas on to some external agency, acting either directly or indirectly through forces over which we ourselves never seem to acquire control.

No colonial power acts in the interest of the colonized against its own interest. The British who ruled India were not saints; but they were not villains either. They introduced innovations in law and governance, some of which were mutually beneficial and continue to be of value even after the end of colonial rule. Our present

Constitution owes a great deal to these innovations. The Drafting Committee was attacked more than once for what it borrowed from the Government of India Act of 1935. The Constitution that came to be adopted has a much closer affinity with that Act than with the *Manusmriti* or any other *Dharmashastra*. Dr Ambedkar recognized this, and he did not hesitate to speak his mind on it.

In his closing speech to the Constituent Assembly, he drew pointed attention to the burden of responsibility that the cessation of colonial rule was going to place on the leaders of independent India. 'By independence, we have lost the excuse of blaming the British for anything going wrong. If hereafter things go wrong, we will have nobody to blame except ourselves' (*CAD* 1989, XI: 980). The British left more than sixty years ago, but there is no lack of intellectual ammunition among patriotic Indians, of the left as well as the right, to fire at them and other western nations when things go wrong with us.

* * *

The Constitution was designed to serve the needs of a modern society. It looked to the future rather than the past. Its architects did not hesitate to draw upon such elements from the Government of India Act of 1935 as could be adapted to the needs of a free and independent nation. It also drew inspiration from other modern constitutions such as the American, the Australian, and the Irish. Dr Ambedkar did not wish to take India back to its past but to prepare it to take its place in the forefront of the comity of free and independent nations of the modern world.

Rightly or wrongly, he felt the lack of a living democratic tradition in India. Indian society was a society of castes and communities. It was not a society of citizens based on the equal consideration of individuals without regard for caste, creed, or gender. To transform a society of castes and communities into one of citizens would be no easy task. The Constitution could at best provide a legal framework, a necessary but not sufficient condition for such a transformation. It could not by itself conjure into existence the attitudes, dispositions, and sentiments without which the transformation could hardly be effective.

To be effective, constitutional laws have to rest on a substratum of constitutional morality. Could the presence of such a morality be taken for granted in our country? Dr Ambedkar was deeply concerned over the question. 'Constitutional morality,' he said, 'is not a natural sentiment. It has to be cultivated. We must realize that our people are yet to learn it. Democracy in India is only a top-dressing on an Indian soil, which is essentially undemocratic' (Ibid. VII: 38). It is clear that he was speaking not just of Indians as they were under British rule, but as they had been over a very long span of time.

In the absence of constitutional morality, the operation of a Constitution, no matter how carefully written, tends to become arbitrary, erratic, and capricious. It is not possible in a democratic order to insulate completely the domain of law from that of politics. A Constitution such as ours is expected to provide guidance on what should be regulated by the impersonal rule of law and what may be settled by the competition for power among parties, among factions, and among political leaders. It is here that the significance of constitutional morality lies. Without some infusion of constitutional morality among legislators, judges, lawyers, ministers, civil servants, writers, and public intellectuals, the Constitution becomes a plaything of power brokers.

Ours is a very lengthy and elaborate Constitution. This was pointed out in the Constituent Assembly itself. Dr Ambedkar's justification was that the absence of a democratic tradition required the provisions in the Constitution to be written out in much greater detail than in the more mature democracies where there was greater consensus on how democratic institutions should function (Ibid.). Not only were the American and French constitutions very brief compared with ours, but Britain, which had evolved the most successful system of parliamentary democracy, did not have a written constitution. The stronger the presence of constitutional morality, the less need there is to put everything down in black and white.

The Drafting Committee decided not to leave too much to the discretion of future legislatures whose political sagacity could not be taken for granted. 'It follows that it is only where people are saturated with constitutional morality ... that one can take the risk of omitting from the Constitution details of administration and leaving it for the legislature to prescribe them' (Ibid.). The venality of legislatures increasingly brought to light by the media confirms Dr Ambedkar's worst misgivings.

Despite the best efforts of the Drafting Committee to make the Constitution foolproof, it has not been possible to insulate it fully from the vagaries of legislative pressures. No democratic constitution can do without provisions for its own amendment. These provisions were crafted with great care so as to make amendments difficult and not easy. Nevertheless, the amendment provisions have been used liberally. Already in Nehru's time, Rajaji, the most sagacious among the nationalist leaders, was warning against the cavalier use of the amendment provisions. The Constitution has been amended close to a hundred times since its adoption in 1950.

When it comes to amending the Constitution, what seems to count for more than considerations of constitutional morality, is the calculation of numbers. If it has not been amended more frequently, it is in part because getting the numbers together has become increasingly difficult in an era of coalition politics. It is, of course, easier to amend legislative enactments, including Acts of Parliament, than to amend the Constitution. In a state legislature, where there is a clear though unstable majority, getting an amendment through is a relatively easy matter.

It might appear that dissension, discord, and clamour in Parliament would make enactments and amendments difficult. This is true to some extent, but bargains can always be made that benefit members across parties in order to ensure the relatively smooth passage of a bill. What passes through Parliament and what is held back have begun to appear increasingly unpredictable to concerned citizens who watch with dismay parliamentary proceedings on television. There is growing suspicion that legislation is sometimes enacted not in the public interest but in order to accommodate a particular faction, a particular community, or, in the extreme case, even a particular political leader. The leader will, of course, have cleared his ground in advance by softening up power brokers of various political persuasions.

* * *

India survives as a democracy despite many predictions to the contrary at the time of independence and in the years that immediately followed (Guha 2007: xi–xvii). Dr Ambedkar himself had expressed anxiety about the prospects of democracy in his closing speech to the Constituent Assembly. He pointed to the fragility of democratic institutions in the country and the adverse social environment in which they would have to operate. Looking to the future, he asked, 'What would happen to her democratic Constitution? Will she be able to maintain it or will she lose it again?' (*CAD* 1989, XI: 978).

India's record since independence has confounded the doubters in many respects. Democracy has shown great resilience in the country, and its capacity for survival is no longer seriously questioned by many. Elections are held periodically, and they are reasonably free and fair. The legitimacy of opposition is acknowledged, and opposition parties lead a vigorous existence. The legislatures conduct their affairs openly, despite the disorder and allegations of horse-trading. The courts enjoy a fair measure of public trust despite mounting suspicions of venality against judges. Even the administrative executive has to act with circumspection when it violates the rule of law, which it does frequently if not regularly. There is freedom of movement and assembly and, most important of all, freedom of expression: nobody will deny that in India people are free to speak their minds or that they express themselves openly and vigorously.

Whereas sixty years ago, there was anxiety about the survival of democracy, today its continued existence has come to be taken for granted. With India's successful economic performance during the last couple of decades, the country is now held up as a success story for democracy by leaders of many countries, including the

United States. It is even said that if democracy does not work in India, it does not have much of a future in the world.

Today, the question is no longer whether democracy will survive in India, but what kind of democracy it will be. Here I would like to introduce the distinction I have made earlier between 'constitutional democracy' and 'populist democracy' (Béteille 1999: 2591; 2000a: 194–6), and to argue that democracy has survived in India not by adhering strictly to the ideal of a constitutional democracy but by moving away from it towards a more populist form.

It is, of course, well known that democracy has many forms. Moreover, in our times the magic of the word 'democracy' is such that many dictatorships would like to present themselves as democracies of the purest kind. The twentieth century made us familiar with the idea of 'peoples' democracy' which is very different from the kind of democracy to which the Indian Constitution sought to give shape. The idea behind a 'peoples' democracy', so far as I have been able to understand it, is to put the interests of the people, viewed as a more or less homogeneous body, above considerations of constitutional procedure, or, as some would put it, above 'mere legality'. The proponents of populism do not in principle deny the value of rules and procedures, only they are prepared to override them when that can be justified by an appeal to the interests of the people.

It would be a mistake to underestimate the strong appeal of populist democracy, particularly in countries that were latecomers to development and without the strong foundations for the rule of law required for the success of a constitutional democracy. Lenin and Mao were among the great political innovators of modern times, and no one can deny the admiration, not to say veneration, they inspired among ordinary people in their respective countries and outside. Yet they, and particularly Mao, had little regard for the procedural forms essential to constitutional democracy which their followers have dismissed as 'bourgeois democracy'. In the Soviet Union and the People's Republic of China, 'constitutional legality' had often to make way for 'revolutionary legality'.

A strong argument against constitutional democracy has been that it gives the advantage to the bourgeoisie or the middle class over other social classes and hence it makes equality, which many view as coterminous with democracy itself, an early casualty. This argument has been made repeatedly by left intellectuals, and it cannot be easily dismissed. In India it is becoming increasingly common for the elected representatives of the people to claim supremacy for Parliament over the other organs of the state, on the ground that it is closer to the people by virtue of its class composition than the other two organs. But no constitutional democracy can function without a significant place given in it to a professionally trained and qualified judiciary and civil service, and these are both components of the middle class rather than the working class or the peasantry. It is pointless to castigate judges and civil servants for their middle-class affiliation when their very profession makes them members of that class. But one can hardly conclude from this that civil servants, judges, or even legislators can act only in the interest of the class to which they belong and never in the general interest.

Writing about Germany on the eve of Hitler's ascendance, Alan Bullock (1993: 428) observed: 'While democratic ideas had failed to take firm root in Germany, the concept of a *Rechtsstaat*, a constitutional state, guaranteeing the rule of law and judicial independence, was accepted in principle in Prussia and other German states from the end of the eighteenth century and had been consolidated in practice during the nineteenth.'

With us, the tendency since independence has been the opposite. Here the democratic urge for equality appears to have gripped the political imagination far more firmly than the idea of the constitutional state.

As I have noted, constitutionalism, because of its alleged class bias, has always been viewed with a degree of mistrust in the tradition of Leninist politics, and that tradition continues to have an appeal among important sections of the Indian intelligentsia. Dr Ambedkar, who was well aware of this, did not shrink from expressing his disdain for it either within or outside the Constituent Assembly.

In his closing speech he said, 'The Communist Party wants a Constitution based upon the principle of the Dictatorship of the Proletariat. They condemn the constitution because it is based on parliamentary democracy' (*CAD* 1989, XI: 975). Today, of course the communist parties are somewhat different from what they were in Lenin's or even Mao's time. They have learnt to operate through the parliamentary system and to co-exist with other parties, not only when they are in opposition but also when they are in government. In a country like India it is impossible for the communists, even when they are in authority, to practice 'revolutionary legality' without let or hindrance. But their fascination for its ideals makes their attachment to constitutional legality at best half-hearted. Their earlier hostility towards constitutionalism has been replaced by a more ambivalent disposition, due in part to the divisions and subdivisions within the communist movement itself.

Constitutional democracy acts through a prescribed division of functions between legislature, executive, and judiciary. Populist democracy regards such division of functions as cumbersome and arbitrary impediments that act overtly or covertly against the will of the people. Populism sets great store by achieving political objectives swiftly and directly through mass mobilization in the form of rallies, demonstrations, and other spectacular displays of mass support. Constitutionalism, on the other hand, seeks to achieve its objectives methodically through the established institutions of governance.

The Leninist and Maoist traditions of mass mobilization are not the only inspirations for populism in Indian politics. There is also the Gandhian tradition of civil disobedience used with great effect during the nationalist movement. No two leaders could be more different than Lenin and Gandhi. Lenin considered violence as a legitimate instrument of politics whereas for Gandhi non-violence was the supreme virtue in both principle and practice. However, one has to make a distinction between Gandhi and those who have acted in his name after his passing, which happened before the Constitution was adopted. No one has shown—or can be expected to show—the restraint and moral discipline of which he was the great exemplar.

Dr Ambedkar appealed against the politics of mobilization in the altered conditions created by the Constitution. He conceded that such politics may have been necessary to bring about a change of regime but that it could no longer be justified under the new regime. What does it mean to adopt a system of constitutional democracy?

> It means that we must abandon the method of civil disobedience, non-cooperation and satyagraha. When there was no way left for constitutional methods for economic and social objectives, there was a great deal of justification for unconstitutional methods. But where constitutional methods are open, there can be no justification for these unconstitutional methods. These methods are nothing but the Grammar of Anarchy and the sooner they are abandoned, the better for us. (Ibid.: 978)

It is no small achievement of Indian democracy that, despite the economic crises and social turbulence the country has undergone, the Constitution has remained in place for close to six decades. It has been amended many times, and there have been those who have said that it has been defaced and defiled (Palkhivala 1974). Yet it remains as an important signpost for the judiciary, and also the legislature.

How deeply has the Constitution influenced the outlook of ordinary citizens in India? Dr Ambedkar had hoped that our people would learn the lessons of constitutional morality in course of time. How much have they in fact learnt? Not very long ago, a prominent member of the Union cabinet had said, 'I know that most members of Parliament see the constitution for the first time when they take an oath on it' (quoted in Guha 2007: 660). This does not provide much comfort to those who cling to the belief that constitutional values will soon come to prevail in India.

* * *

The infirmity of constitutional values is brought into relief when the political system undergoes a crisis. It has undergone many crises, large and small, since independence, and has come out of them more or less successfully. But there can be little doubt that the long-term effect of these crises has been a weakening rather than a strengthening of constitutional values, at least as these were conceived of at the time of independence.

The Emergency of 1975–7 and the events that preceded and followed it clearly revealed the connection between anarchy and the abuse of power as two forces that feed on the weakness of constitutional morality (Béteille 2000b). It did not last very long, but it left deep scars on India's democratic political system. Those who supported the Emergency pointed to the turmoil and disorder, bordering on anarchy, let loose by various popular movements in Gujarat, Bihar, and elsewhere (Dhar 2000: 223–68, 371–406). Those who opposed it—and they prevailed in the end—pointed to the naked abuse of power and the flagrant violation of the spirit, and sometimes even the letter, of the Constitution during it. The Emergency was bad in itself; to add to its own inherent evil, it created an opposition which legitimized a populist disregard of established institutions that has spread its roots in the Indian soil.

In the summer of 1975, the prime minister, in the face of mounting social and political turmoil, lost her nerve and declared a state of Emergency. The Emergency was meant to quell the turmoil through strong executive action and to secure the compliance of the legislature and the judiciary to the executive. It made the arbitrary use of power and its increasing misuse inevitable. Professor P.N. Dhar, who was then the prime minister's principal secretary, has documented the way in which the centre of decision-making shifted from the Prime Minister's Office to the prime minister's house (Dhar 2000: 300–51).

Power began to be exercised from the prime minister's house with little regard for constitutional proprieties, not to speak of constitutional morality. It would be surprising if it were otherwise. From his strategic position in the prime minister's house, her younger son, Sanjay Gandhi, who enjoyed no constitutional authority of any kind, took decisions that caused bewilderment and fear among ministers, legislators, and judges. Many of them complied with a show of servility far in excess of what was required, revealing to the world at large the infirmity of constitutional values at the top of the political hierarchy.

Those who remained loyal to Mrs Gandhi point out that the Emergency did not last very long, and that it did not hit people equally hard in all parts of the country. They also point out that it was Mrs Gandhi herself who lifted it and called for elections at a time when the political pressure for such a move was not very strong. Her manner throughout the period showed that she was not at ease with herself. Nevertheless, it revealed deep fault lines in the political order. The ascendance of Sanjay Gandhi showed how fragile constitutional proprieties are in the face of personal loyalties and family attachments. Mrs Gandhi's conduct made it clear that in the end she could trust neither her cabinet nor her party, nor even her secretariat, but only her son and his cronies.

It will be difficult to exaggerate the significance of family, kinship, and community in Indian society. Loyalties to family and community are not dictated merely by personal interest; they arise out of moral compulsions that are deeply rooted in Indian social values. It will be a mistake to deny the moral basis of the obligations of family, kinship, and community. But the moral basis of these obligations is different from the basis of constitutional morality. Problems arise when the loyalties of kinship and community are allowed to distort and override the demands of constitutional government.

The salience of the dynastic principle and its pernicious hold over Indian politics has been noted by many (for example, Malhotra 2003). The subject has led to endless moralizing but not much systematic analysis. Here the Congress party and the pre-eminent position in it of the Nehru–Gandhi family has received the most attention nationally and internationally (Guha 2007: 575–602). From the record, it will be difficult to deny Mr Nehru's own commitment to constitutional norms and proprieties. But the story changes after him. The Emergency appears as a turning point because it brought out Mrs Gandhi's failure to trust anyone outside her own family. When one son died, she brought in the other, and thereafter her family came to occupy an unassailable position within the Congress party.

Critics of the dynastic principle have found it natural to blame the Nehru–Gandhi family for refusing to yield its pre-eminent position in Indian politics. But this would be to take a short-sighted and one-sided view of the matter. It is a truism that in a democracy the followers get the leaders they deserve. How has it come about that India's premier political party, the party of the nationalist movement, from the highest office-bearers to the lowest rank-and-file member, has become so abjectly dependent for its survival and success on one single family? We will fail to understand the nature of the problem if we refuse to recognize the fact that millions of Indians continue to believe that the natural succession to high office lies within the family. It is neither individual nor institutional charisma, but the charisma of the family that prevails.

The Nehru–Gandhi family may be the most striking example of the dynastic principle but it is by no means the only example of it in Indian politics. Inder Malhotra, who has been a keen observer of the Indian political scene since Nehru's time, has given many examples of what he calls 'mini' and 'midi' dynasties in the states. He too has related the operation of the principle to the strength of family ties and family obligations among the people of the subcontinent (Malhotra 2003: 25–6). No political institution, whether a legislature or a party, can be sustained without trust in its leadership. It seems that millions of Indians are more willing to repose their trust on a member of the leader's family than on a person of proven experience and ability but unrelated to him. This raises the larger question of how much trust they have in the institutions of democracy as compared with their trust in family, kinship, and community.

* * *

I would now like to return to the point made earlier that anarchy and the abuse of power are but two sides of the same coin. Each is in its own way antithetical to constitutional morality.

Without in any way extenuating Mrs Gandhi's toleration, not to say endorsement, of the abuse of power from the prime minister's house during the Emergency, it is necessary to turn now to the other side of the coin. The Emergency did not come out of the blue in the summer of 1975. It came under conditions of unprecedented disorder and turmoil in the country. Perhaps Mrs Gandhi called for the Emergency because she lost her nerve, or perhaps there was an inherently authoritarian strain in her personality waiting for an occasion to find expression. Whatever may have been the flaws in Mrs Gandhi's personality, we cannot afford to ignore the social and political conditions that were the immediate antecedents of the Emergency. As P.N. Dhar (2000: 373) looking back on the events wrote: 'Indeed the Emergency as well as the JP movement further weakened the institutions essential for genuine democracy. Both these events reduced respect for the rule of law: the Emergency by an authoritarian disregard for legal norms and the JP movement by rationalizing and glamorizing the defiance of all authority.'

Opposition to Mrs Gandhi's government was building up in many parts of the country from 1972 onwards although the government enjoyed a comfortable majority in Parliament. The movement against it was already gathering strength when Jayaprakash Narayan, known throughout the country as JP, took over its leadership. JP was a leader of outstanding political and moral stature, who was known for his integrity and selflessness and who had enjoyed the esteem of an earlier generation of nationalists, including Jawaharlal Nehru. His re-entry into the political arena galvanized the opposition against Mrs Gandhi.

JP had had an interesting political formation and career. He had been influenced successively by Marxism and Gandhism, and these two influences combined in him to create a revolutionary movement of a very distinctive kind. When he took over the movement against Mrs Gandhi, he was hoping to carry the masses forward not simply to a change in the government within the existing regime but to a change of the regime itself.

As the rallies, *dharnas* and *bandhs* were gathering momentum, JP gave the call for sampurna kranti. That became the rallying cry for the movement against Mrs Gandhi's government. Sampurna kranti or total revolution (literally total struggle) was JP's term for a comprehensive social revolution that would purge Indian society of all its accumulated ills, and recreate it on a higher moral plane. Where total revolution is the issue, one cannot remain confined to constitutional methods and shrink from the use of extra-constitutional ones.

Dr Ambedkar might argue the case for constitutional morality, but there are others who feel that a revolutionary morality stands superior to it.

Though influenced by Marxism in his early years, JP had moved beyond the class struggle. In his effort to achieve total revolution, he sought to mobilize youth power or *yuva shakti* as the driving force. Youth power had been used earlier in western countries such as France and the USA in moderate doses, and with devastating effect in China during the Great Proletarian Cultural Revolution of 1966 onwards. It did not destroy constitutional practices and conventions in India, but it certainly fostered an attitude of disdain towards them.

Impressed by the success of the students working through the Nav Nirman Samiti in Gujarat, JP decided to carry the movement into his home state of Bihar. The students there were agitating on various issues such as shortages, inflation, unemployment, fees, and scholarships when they sought JP's intervention to bring the state government to its knees and get the state legislature dissolved. Conditions had become unsettled and there was tension in the air. It was hoped that the legislators could be persuaded to resign in large numbers. When persuasion failed, JP gave a call for the *gherao* of the assembly and the residences of the members of the legislative assembly (MLAs). He himself led a procession to the secretariat where he staged a dharna.

The JP movement of 1974–5 dismayed some, but it elated others. It brought in a new sense of expectation. The expectation, shared by many at the time, and particularly the youth, was that democracy in India was about to acquire a new lease of life and, even, that a new kind of democracy was about to be born. But this new democracy would not be a constitutional but a populist one. I would go so far as to say that the spirit of populism, never too far from the surface, came out into the open and invested the political system with new energy.

The capacity to mobilize large masses of people for rallies and demonstrations encouraged political leaders to disregard the rule of law. The opposition parties were not alone in organizing rallies.

If JP could attract huge crowds in Patna, Mrs Gandhi could do the same in Delhi. On her side, the organization of rallies was put in the care of her younger son who had taken over the leadership of the Youth Congress. Sanjay took little care to conceal his disdain for constitutional proprieties, relying on muscle power instead.

Competitive populism reached its high-water mark in the summer of 1975. No political party, whether of the left, the right, or the centre, can disown responsibility for its rise. All political parties, including the smallest, know that in India it does not take much to organize a rally of a hundred thousand persons. Rallies have a social as well as a political side, and sometimes they have the atmosphere of a carnival. Nor are rallies organized only by political parties. They may be organized by religious bodies, by farmers, and by caste formations of various kinds. The recent organization of rallies by the Gujjar community in Rajasthan is a case in point. Its leaders had no doubt that they were only using the most effective means available to exercise their democratic rights.

Democracy rests on a delicate balance between the rule of law and the rule of numbers. Populism invokes the principle of numbers, and constitutionalism the principle of legality. No constitutional order can continue for long if it has no support among the people, and a populist movement in course of time develops its own rules and conventions. At the same time, the way in which the balance is attained between the attachment to numbers and the attachment to legality differs from one democratic system to another and, within the same system, from one phase in its life to the next. In India there has been a clear shift since 1977 in favour of numerical support. This can be seen from the decisions taken in Parliament, where the calculation of numbers acquires priority over legislative consistency.

Looking back on the events that came immediately before the Emergency, one cannot help remembering the wise words of Dr Ambedkar's closing speech in the Constituent Assembly. The attainment of independence did not lead to the rejection of the Grammar of Anarchy but, in course of time, to its more extensive use. Neither the ruling party nor the parties in opposition paid much heed to the restraints required by constitutional morality or the principle of legality. The Congress felt that it had the numbers in Parliament, and the parties behind the JP movement felt that they could paralyse the government by bringing their supporters on to the streets. The ruling party in its turn brought out the thugs of the Youth Congress. When that did not work, the government declared a state of Emergency.

No one can deny that in declaring the Emergency Mrs Gandhi strayed from the path of constitutional rectitude. It will be generally agreed that among all the prime ministers of independent India, Indira Gandhi was the most repressive and the most ruthless. But she was not animated by the kind of destructive ideological passion that caused so much violence in the USSR under Lenin and Stalin and in China under Mao. The nationalist tradition in Indian politics was very different from the Bolshevik and the Communist traditions, and it is doubtful that she could ever fully put behind her the examples of Gandhi and Nehru. So in the end she did call off the Emergency and try to meet her constitutional obligations by a return to electoral politics.

* * *

Dr Ambedkar was well aware that the successful operation of democracy would require not only the creation of a new political order but also the creation of a corresponding social order. Would the prevalent social order in India be able to rise to the challenges presented by the new Constitution? He had misgivings about this, and developments in government and politics since his time have shown that his misgivings were not without foundation.

The operation of a modern democracy rests upon three interlinked components. These are (i) state, (ii) citizenship, and (iii) mediating institutions (Béteille 2000a: 172–97). Each is important in its own way, but it is only in their mutual relations that they provide the basis for a democratic social and political order. Human history has witnessed many different kinds of state: the tribal state, the feudal state, the absolutist state, the imperial state, and so on. Our concern here is with the constitutional state governed by the impersonal rule of law, what the Germans call the Reschtsstaat. A constitutional state, by its very nature, sets clearly defined limits to its own authority.

What is not always recognized is that the constitutional state can operate only through an apparatus which is a system of graded authority. Populism of the kind represented by the call for sampurna kranti is on the other hand emancipationist and antinomian in its outlook. It regards all systems of graded authority as bastions against the immediate and pressing needs of the people. The gradation of authority and the abuse of power are, of course, two different things, but in a populist perspective they are easily confused, and the functionaries of the state become the natural targets of the hostility against privilege.

Citizenship represents the pole opposite to the state in a constitutional democracy. The concept of citizenship is a modern one. During the colonial period, Indians were subjects and not citizens, and traditional Indian society was a society of castes and communities rather than of citizens. The modern concept of citizenship is an individualizing as well as a universalizing one. The rights of citizenship are the rights of individuals, without consideration of race, caste, creed, or gender, and they are the same for all Indian citizens.

Contrary to the hopes and aspirations of many in the Constituent Assembly, Indian society has not ceased to be a society of castes and communities. Democratic politics has in many ways strengthened collective identities at the expense of the identity of the individual as citizen. Here, what Dr Ambedkar had said about majorities and minorities applies in a general way to all forms of collective identity. He had said, 'It is wrong for the majority to deny the existence of minorities. It is equally wrong for the minorities to perpetuate themselves' (*CAD* 1989, VII: 39). The vicious cycle of discrimination and self-perpetuation continues unabated.

The two poles of the state and the citizen are linked together by organizations, associations, institutions, and interpersonal networks of many different kinds. It is these mediating structures that hold society together and give to each society its distinctive character.

Among the diverse arrangements, I would like to single out those that I describe as institutions. An institution is a social arrangement with a distinct identity, a distinct internal structure and culture, and a life span extending beyond the lives of its individual members. Mediating institutions themselves are of many different kinds, of which only some, and not all, are of central significance to the functioning of a constitutional democracy.

The mediating institutions that I have in mind are open and secular institutions, homologous in their character to the constitutional state and citizenship. They are very different from the institutions of kinship, caste, and religion that formed the basis of state and society in traditional India. They are open in the sense that membership in them is independent of considerations of race, caste, and gender, and they are secular in the sense that their internal arrangements are not regulated by religious rules or religious authorities.

The antinomian currents by which populist democracy is propelled find themselves at odds not only with the institutions of the state but, more generally, with public institutions and their structures of authority. Obvious examples of public institutions that have had to withstand the currents of populist movements in India are its universities and colleges. Their organization and functioning have been affected for long stretches at a time in many parts of the country, and in some cases they have been seriously, and perhaps irreversibly, impaired.

University and college students are ideally positioned for mobilization in support of populist causes. They are impressionable and idealistic, and they can be absent from their allotted work for long periods without risk of having to suffer any immediate consequences. If the movement is sufficiently large in its scope, it is likely to be joined by their teachers who provide it with additional momentum. Ordinarily, the forces of law and order treat such movements more indulgently than movements by workers or peasants. But if there is violence from one side, it may be matched by violence from the other.

*   *   *

Constitutional morality would stand impoverished if it failed to accommodate the principle of civil disobedience. Under the leadership of Mahatma Gandhi, civil disobedience became the cornerstone of the nationalist movement, and it would be unreasonable to expect it to fade away from the Indian imagination. Whenever large popular movements are organized against the government, the idea of civil disobedience tends to be invoked. This happened at the time of the JP movement, and it was not the last time that it happened. The historical association with Gandhi gives a special appeal to any movement that presents itself as an act of civil disobedience.

Dr Ambedkar had no doubt been right to point out that the context of popular protest had changed with the passage from colonial rule to self-rule. When they were ruled by an alien power, the people of India had limited means by which to influence their rulers. With independence, the rulers and the ruled became in some sense one and the same people. The impediments to being heard by the rulers and even calling them to account were no longer as unassailable as in the past. Where ordinary measures for the articulation of discontent had become accessible, extraordinary ones would no longer be required.

While independence was no doubt a watershed in the life of the nation, things have not stood still since it was attained. I have referred to those days as days of high expectations. Not surprisingly, many of those expectations could not be met. The people of India have gradually learnt that their own elected leaders can be as deaf to their pleas as the ones who came from outside. Sometimes they have shown themselves to be even more venal and self-serving than the British who ruled India. Or perhaps, because Indians had developed such high expectations of their own elected leaders, they lost patience with them more quickly and became more peremptory with their demands on them.

The strength or weakness of constitutional morality in contemporary India has to be understood in the light of a cycle of escalating demands from the people and the callous response of successive governments to those demands. In a parliamentary democracy, the obligations of constitutional morality are expected to be equally binding on the government and the opposition. In India, the same political party treats these obligations very differently when it is in office and when it is out of it. This has contributed greatly to the popular perception of our political system as being amoral.

In a political system in which the principal parties, whether in office or in opposition, have shown themselves to be venal and self-serving, it would be folly to close the door on civil disobedience. But civil disobedience, as no one understood better than Gandhi, is not a panacea, and it does not come without a price. Gandhi was unyielding in his view that civil disobedience had to be non-violent, and he was prepared to eat humble pie and call it off when it took a violent turn.

Reflective advocates of it have pointed out that civil disobedience cannot be a matter only of disobedience, it must also be civil. For Gandhi, civil disobedience, as a form of non-violent resistance, was essentially a moral force. It required the cultivation of distinctive moral qualities to pass muster as a form of non-violent resistance. In particular, it required among its practitioners a habit of obedience to the laws, including inconvenient ones (Gandhi 1961). Civil disobedience, in this view, cannot be aimed against inconvenient laws, but only against unjust ones. It is another matter that leaders of public protest in India have never found it difficult to present inconvenient laws as unjust ones.

The virtue of civility is an important component of constitutional morality. It calls for tolerance, restraint, and mutual accommodation in public life. Civility is a moderating influence which acts against the extremes of ideological politics. 'It restrains the exercise of power by the powerful and restrains obstruction and violence by those who do not have power but who wish to have it' (Shils 1997: 4). Civility is an important condition for the smooth operation of public institutions such as universities. Universities in the modern world have learnt to live with protests, agitations, and demonstrations. But when these acquire an adversarial or an antinomian form as a matter of habit, as they did on the eve of the Emergency and in its aftermath, something goes out of the life of the university as a centre of science and scholarship. It is against this kind of possibility that Dr Ambedkar had issued his warning about the Grammar of Anarchy.

Civil disobedience may take a persuasive or a coercive form (Haksar 1986). Gandhi certainly did not intend it to be used as an instrument of coercion. He agonized all the time that the movements he led might degenerate into anarchy and violence; he was no less mindful than Dr Ambedkar of the destructive potential of the grammar of anarchy. Yet, it will be hard to deny that agitations, demonstrations, and rallies undertaken in the name of civil disobedience have increasingly become coercive not only in their consequences but even in their intentions. What Dr Ambedkar had hoped would die down after independence has in fact become intensified since 1977.

There are responsible citizens who would make a case for mass rallies and demonstrations even though they are fully aware that they can become coercive. They say that they are forced to take the risk of anarchy and disorder where they know that the authorities, whether in the government or in public institutions such as universities, pay no heed to reasonable persuasion but respond only to threats. It is a fact that in recent decades public authorities have tended to respond more readily to threats than to persuasion even to the point of violating their own norms. As I have said, citizens alone cannot be expected to adhere to the norms of constitutional morality if the state persistently disregards those norms.

The JP movement of 1974–5 was the culmination of a period of uncertainty and disorder. The social and political conditions for its emergence had been growing in various parts of the country for some time. Nevertheless, it can be seen as a watershed in India's social and political life. When the Emergency was withdrawn, the political system did not return to the status quo ante. The new government that assumed office after Mrs Gandhi's defeat adopted an ambitious social agenda. That agenda was dictated by the promises its leaders had made in the period that led to the Emergency and during the elections that brought them to power after it. It was too ambitious for it or for any government with its resources to fulfil.

The new government ran into difficulty almost immediately after it assumed office. It was a coalition of too many parties whose diverse constituents exerted contradictory pressures on it. A clash of personalities soon appeared on the surface, and the politics of principles was overtaken by the politics of patronage.

As I have pointed out, the JP movement, like populist movements in general, was emancipationist and antinomian. These two closely related aims and tendencies did not die down with the end of the movement. They have become lodged in our political culture as an integral element of it. They cannot be wished out of existence, no matter how much they might conflict with the principles of legality on which the Constitution is based.

Populism has not only become a part of our democracy, but from time to time it puts forward its demands in a very imperious form. When that happens, many naturally feel that the Constitution itself is under threat. At the same time, no serious move has ever been made to discard the Constitution, or to design a different one to replace it.

Even during the darkest days of the Emergency, Mrs Gandhi retained a residual attachment to the Constitution, and JP's defiance of it in the cause of total revolution was at best half-hearted. Our politicians may devise ingenious ways of getting round the Constitution and violating its rules from time to time, but they do not like to see the open defiance of it by others. In that sense the Constitution has come to acquire a significant symbolic value among Indians. But the currents of populism run deep in the country's political life, and they too have their own moral compulsions. It would appear therefore that the people of India are destined to oscillate endlessly between the two poles of constitutionalism and populism without ever discarding the one or the other.

References

Béteille, André. 1981. *The Backward Classes and the New Social Order.* New Delhi: Oxford University Press.
———. 1987. *The Idea of Natural Inequality and Other Essays.* New Delhi: Oxford University Press, 2nd edn.
———. 1999. 'Citizenship, State and Civil Society', *Economic and Political Weekly*, vol. xxxiv, no. 36, pp. 2566–91.

————. 2000a. *Antinomies of Society*. New Delhi: Oxford
University Press.

————. 2000b. 'Anarchy and the Abuse of Power', *Economic and
Political Weekly*, vol. xxxv, no. 10, pp. 779–83.

————. 2002. *Equality and Universality*. New Delhi: Oxford
University Press.

Bullock, Alan. 1993. *Hitler and Stalin*. New York: Vintage Books.

Constituent Assembly Debates (CAD). 1989. *Official Report*. New Delhi:
Government of India, vols VII and XI.

Dhar, P.N. 2000. *Indira Gandhi, the 'Emergency' and Indian
Democracy*. New Delhi: Oxford University Press.

Gandhi, M.K. 1961. *Non-Violent Resistance*. New York: Shocken
Books.

Guha, Ramachandra. 2007. *India After Gandhi*. London: Macmillan.

Haksar, Vinit. 1986. *Civil Disobedience, Threats and Offers*.
New Delhi: Oxford University Press.

Malhotra, Inder. 2003. *Dynasties of India and Beyond*. New Delhi:
HarperCollins.

Palkhivala, Nani A. 1974. *Our Constitution Defaced and Defiled*.
New Delhi: Macmillan.

Shils, Edward. 1997. *The Virtue of Civility*. Indianapolis:
Liberty Fund.

5

Can Rights Undermine Trust?
How Institutions Work and Why They Fail

I would like to discuss first the importance of rights in social life, and then the social significance of trust. My argument will be that rights and trust are both indispensable constituents of collective life. No society can function without an acknowledged distribution of rights among its constituent members. But a component of trust, or a fiduciary component as one might call it, is no less important for the well-being of collective life.

An excessive emphasis on trust may lead to the rights of some members of society being ignored and hence repeatedly violated. Today this is a common predicament of women entrapped within the traditional family; examples may be found from other areas of social life. At the same time, the continuous assertion of rights by the members of society, either individually or collectively, undermines the fiduciary basis of society. This is a common feature of public life in contemporary India, and the example that comes to my mind first and foremost is the Indian university today. The erosion of trust makes it difficult for individuals to contribute fruitfully to the collective endeavour.

The fiduciary component operates at every level of society and in every kind of social arrangement from domestic institutions to financial markets. But where there is trust, there is also a potential for malfeasance or breach of trust which cannot be resolved without recourse to rights. We have recently had dramatic reminders of the consequences of the failure of trust in financial markets in the United States and elsewhere. At a different level, there are daily reminders of the same phenomenon that come from the divorce courts.

It is a truism for the sociologist that no society can be sustained without rights and without trust. A major task of social analysis is to examine the balance that exists between the two. The importance of this balance tends to be overlooked by those who are preoccupied with only one of the two, to the neglect of the other.

The balance between rights and trust is a complex matter, and it is rarely a completely stable one, particularly in a changing society such as ours is today. It will be a mistake to presume that rights and trust always reinforce each other; nor, of course, can we argue that they always act against each other. The balance between the two is never the same in every society, or for all time. It varies from one society to another, and even from one domain to another within the same society. How this balance operates in a changing society is a subject of some importance that has not received its due attention from students of society and politics in India.

The concept of rights is a difficult one, and the concept of trust both difficult and elusive. One can of course examine the contrasting roles of rights and trust in society as a whole, or in one or more of its various domains. My view is that we will get a better sense of each of the two by viewing it not in isolation but in its dialectical relationship with the other.

My emphasis will be on institutions which are social arrangements of a particular kind (Béteille 2000a: 153–97). An institution, as I understand it, is an enduring arrangement of roles and relationships with a more or less distinct identity and with boundaries that mark it off from its environment and from other institutions of its own kind or some other kind. Institutions are of various kinds. Some are quite small and others are very large. The family is an institution; a school, a university, a hospital, a laboratory, a court of law, and a bank are all examples of institutions as well. Anyone who is interested in institutions must ask how they endure and what enables them to outlive the individuals who are their members at any particular time.

It is a truism that the roles and relationships that define a family, a college, or even a political party cannot operate outside of a certain framework of rights that define, support, and limit the activities of its members. But can the family, the college, or the party survive and endure as an institution in the absence of mutual trust among its members, or when that trust undergoes steady and irreversible decline?

* * *

The language of rights has acquired a general and almost irresistible appeal in our time, while the language of trust has taken a back seat. This has had to do more with new developments in politics than in law. This, in my view, was not always the case. Gandhi, who was a trained lawyer and as such fully conversant with the language of rights, was inclined to use the language of trust extensively, particularly when it came to the reconstitution of Indian society (Bose 1962; Gandhi 1962). The language of rights has increasingly acquired a radical colour whereas a conservative, not to say reactionary, colour has been assigned to the language of trust. The developments in political and intellectual life since independence that have led to this outcome are too complex to be discussed on this occasion. Suffice it to say that these developments have had a worldwide reach, and have not all originated within the country. International agencies now play an active part in promoting the language of rights, particularly in what they call the less developed countries.

At least in India, the increasing use of the language of rights in public discussion and debate is giving the word 'right' a more capacious and flexible meaning than is ordinarily given to it by the Constitution and the law (Dworkin 1984: 150–205). Its use is becoming more a matter of politics than of law, a subject more of political contest than for legal resolution. If our judges take their cue from the politicians—as some of them seem inclined to do—there will be long-term consequences for the operation of the legal system.

Whereas in the past those seeking to promote a particular programme might ask for the adoption of a new policy, they are more likely now to call for the creation of a new right (Béteille 2005). The demand for a new right seems to infuse a greater sense of urgency than the call for a new policy. Advocacy groups have outdone the political parties in these matters. There are many more such groups now than there were in the early decades of independence, and some of them, unlike political parties in general, have an international reach which adds greatly to their resources and their ability to pursue their agenda.

The Constitution that was adopted in 1950 in the wake of independence provided the architecture of a republican state. It was designed to be different from an imperial or a colonial state. Under colonial rule, Indians were not citizens but subjects: as Nirad C. Chaudhuri (1951) memorably observed in the Dedication of his *Autobiography*, the British Empire conferred subjecthood but withheld citizenship. The republican constitution adopted on independence sought to transform a nation of subjects into one of citizens. The creation of citizenship is a long and arduous process that cannot be accomplished in a day or a decade by the provisions of a constitution, no matter how ample and extensive (Marshall 1977; Béteille 2000a: 181–4). But those provisions nevertheless play a significant part in changing the attitudes and orientations of people.

Citizenship cannot be effective or meaningful without the provision of rights for the citizen. Part II of the Constitution is entitled 'Citizenship' and Part III is devoted to 'Fundamental Rights'. The fundamental rights were extensive to begin with and additions have been made to them by amendment of the Constitution. These rights of citizenship give to each and every Indian a legal standing that is very different from what he or she had in the past. At the same time, it is important to remember that a person's legal standing is only a part, and often a very small part, of his general social standing.

The rights of citizenship are important, first and foremost, as a shield against the arbitrary use of power by the state and its functionaries. The modern state has many powers and it is always hungry for more power. Its functionaries are not notable for using those powers justly or in moderation. The citizen needs some protection from the misuse of state power. The rights of citizenship may not provide a great deal of protection to the ordinary Indian, but how important they are may be appreciated by a comparison with China or the erstwhile Soviet Union where such rights are or were rarely acknowledged or respected.

In any society which adopts a new constitution and a new framework of relations between citizens and state, it is not enough to create extensive rights for the citizens. What is equally, if not more, important is to create a consciousness among citizens so that they are aware of their rights and the ways in which they can exercise them. Creating new rights for citizens and giving them an awareness of their rights are two different things, and the gap between them was particularly large when the Constitution was first adopted. The majority of Indians were unlettered; large numbers of them lived in small and isolated villages; and even in the larger cities many were unaware of what the rights of citizenship meant for them. Things have changed somewhat in the last sixty years, but awareness of the rights of citizenship is still very uneven in the population of the country.

Nobody can gainsay the importance of making people aware of their rights and the ways to exercise them, or the difficulty of the task in a large and somewhat disorderly society which is both deeply divided and highly stratified. These tasks cannot be left entirely to the constituted authorities of the state such as the legislature or the judiciary. Education for citizenship is an important requirement. It is an arduous and protracted process, and many institutions and agencies in addition to the state contribute to it.

A large number of social movements have emerged in the course of the last few decades, partly in response to the disenchantment with the state and its institutions. Some are now inclined to equate these movements with what they call 'civil society'. Their leaders say that, instead of being protectors of the people and their rights, the state has become their oppressor. The Emergency of 1975–7 was a kind of watershed in the life of these movements (Béteille 2000b), although their growth in recent times has been a worldwide phenomenon. Because they seek to secure the rights of the common people, many refer to them as 'grassroots movements'. They have played no small part in bringing the language of rights to the forefront.

A new category of persons, often described as 'rights activists', has become increasingly prominent on the national, and even the international, scene. Rights activists typically operate through non-governmental organizations or NGOs which are now widely described as civil society organizations. Many public-spirited persons in the media, in universities, and some even in the government appear to place more trust in NGOs than in the state for the regeneration of Indian society. And in India, the NGOs receive funds not only from international agencies but from various departments of the government itself. While civil society institutions have an important role in the regeneration of society, the role of the state should not be ignored or minimized.

To the student of civil rights, the co-existence of governmental and non-governmental organizations is a prominent feature of contemporary India. This is not simply a matter of funding but also a matter of personnel. I have known senior bureaucrats to take premature retirement in order to move into the NGO sector, and many able and experienced functionaries of the state become associated with NGOs after retirement. The irony should not be lost that some of the very persons who are suspected and accused of wilfully violating the rights of citizens while in office become champions of those rights after demitting office.

Not all governments are equally well-disposed towards NGOs. The situation in China is strikingly different from our situation. It is in India, and not in China, that the doctrine of 'Let a hundred flowers blossom' corresponds to the reality. It was the same in the Soviet Union as it is now in China, although NGOs have proliferated in many East European countries since the demise of communism. My impression is that the Left Front government in West Bengal has been decidedly less friendly to NGOs than most other state governments in the country. This is because Communist parties are so constituted that they do not welcome organizations that might emerge as parallel agencies for mobilizing popular support.

There can be little doubt that rights activists, advocacy groups, civil society associations, and NGOs have contributed much to the spread of awareness about rights among the people in the last few decades.

But they have not all spoken in the same voice or pursued a single agenda. It is a truism that rights do not signify the same thing in every social situation or to every section of society. A greater awareness of rights may lead to acute conflict between different sections of society, say, different religious or linguistic groups, or different groups of castes, who do not view their respective rights in the same light. The language of rights can then serve as a sword in the conflict between groups of citizens and not just as a shield to protect them from the state.

* * *

Here it is important to make a distinction between civil rights—or the rights of the individual as a citizen—and the rights claimed by or on behalf of particular sections of the population such as the minorities, the backward castes, and women. Needless to say, the claims made on behalf of the individual as a citizen are not identical with the claims made on behalf of particular castes or communities; indeed, the two kinds of claims may come into conflict with each other. At least in India, the language of rights is now used increasingly to assert the claims of socially and economically disadvantaged communities rather those of individuals viewed without consideration of caste, creed, or gender.

The special position of the minorities and the backward castes was acknowledged and even emphasized by the colonial administration in India before independence. Many of the colonial civil servants were keen observers of Indian society and they often took the view that India was a society of castes and communities rather than a nation of citizens. They felt obliged, in the interest of fairness as well as prudence, to adopt special measures to protect and promote the interests of subordinate groups. But the colonial administration viewed these measures as matters of policy rather than right. It is only in the last few decades that the language of rights has come to be increasingly used for advancing the claims of various castes and communities.

In a classic work on the subject, the sociologist T.H. Marshall (1977) traced the development of citizenship in Britain from the eighteenth century to the twentieth. He saw this development as the progressive expansion of rights. The bearers of these rights, in Marshall's view, were individuals and not classes and communities. In fact, he contrasted the divergent tendencies in the development of the rights of citizenship and the divisions of class which, according to him, acted dialectically on each other.

The rights of workers as a class have of course been advanced by trade unions in the advanced industrial countries, particularly in the early stages of the development of capitalism. They are advanced in many countries at the present time as well. But scholars such as Marshall might argue that it was necessary to advance those rights in the early stages of capitalism precisely because workers did not enjoy all the rights of citizenship. Once those rights became available to them, any special case for the rights of the working class became weak.

A class, defined in terms of income, occupation, and employment status, is radically different from a community where membership is acquired by birth. A caste is a classic example of a community of birth. A group defined by mother tongue is another example. For all practical purposes, a religious community may also be viewed as a community of birth even though an individual may renounce the religion of his ancestors and adopt a new one. The movement by an individual from one religion to another is far less common than the movement from one class to another which is in fact a common feature of advanced industrial societies (Erikson and Goldthorpe 1992). The rights of citizenship facilitate the mobility of individuals from one class to another but leave unaltered the individual's membership of the community into which he is born. It is for this reason that policies for improving the conditions of industrial or agricultural workers do not conflict with the rights of citizenship.

Sometimes the collective claims of a class may be presented in such a way as to become conflated with the claims of a religious or other community, and thus become a threat to the claims of the individual as a citizen. This may be illustrated from the experience of the Somali activist and writer, Ayaan Hirsi Ali. When she entered the political arena in the Netherlands, she was naturally drawn to the Labour Party because of its socialist tradition. But she gradually found that the same socialist tradition, with its collectivist bias, stood in her way when she sought to promote the claims of battered and persecuted Muslim women. Her party felt that she should not challenge the authority of the Muslim leadership which regarded the individual rights of those women as less important than the customs and values of the Muslim community. As she saw it, 'Social democracy is grounded in the rights of groups of people, not individuals' (Ali 2007: 296).

The divisions of class continue to be very important in Indian society although not exactly in the same way as those divisions are represented in the trade-union movement or in classical socialist theory. The most important class division in the context of citizenship is not the one between management and labour, or between capitalists and workers, or even between manual and non-manual employees; it is the division between workers in the organized and the unorganized sectors. In India, 90 per cent of manual workers are engaged in work in the unorganized sector, and their conditions of work and life are radically different from those of manual workers in the organized sector, whether in public or in private undertakings.

There has been a sea change in the economic, political, and social conditions of the industrial working class to the extent that it has secured a place in the organized sector. The market situation, work situation, and status situation of its members have improved steadily. Many factors have contributed to this development, including changes in technology, advances in literacy and education, and their own part in organized politics. That section of the working class has in effect become a part of the middle class at least as far as the rights of citizenship go. In the political domain, factory workers act in the same way as, and often in concert with, office workers, school teachers, and others who clearly belong to the middle class. Manual workers in even the lowest-ranked occupations, such as sweepers, enjoy security of employment and livelihood provided they are in the organized sector. Their counterparts in the unorganized sector have been left behind in the process which has led to this convergence.

While the former are able to exercise their rights of citizenship, at least to some extent, those rights are in effect beyond the reach of the latter.

It is not at all my argument that industrial workers have acquired full citizenship in both principle and practice, but only that it is easier to harmonize the claims made on behalf of such workers, whether in the organized or the unorganized sector, with the claims of citizenship. It is not at all clear that the rights of citizenship can be harmonized equally well with the rights claimed on behalf of communities of birth whether based on language, religion, or caste. Increasingly, it is rights of the latter kind that have come to dominate public discourse in recent years. This has been associated with the ascendancy of identity politics over the politics of class.

The ascendancy of identity politics has given a new focus and a new force to the language of rights. It is not as if identity politics was a new phenomenon that came out of the blue in independent India. The politics of caste and community was very much a part of the Indian political scene before independence and was in some ways encouraged by the country's colonial rulers. It did not then have the same scope or the same legitimacy that it has now come to acquire. The British encouraged the religious minorities and the backward castes mainly as a matter of policy. Today their claims are promoted increasingly as matters of right.

I have spoken of the increasing use of the language of rights in the period since independence, and particularly in the aftermath of the Emergency. Its use, however, is not directed mainly to the creation of full citizenship for the truly disadvantaged, the hundreds of millions who labour in the unorganized sector under the most onerous and insecure conditions of life. It is used to a much larger extent in the political contest between the various castes and communities that has come to dominate the political arena today.

Leaders of all political parties have come to realize that it is easier to mobilize electoral support on the basis of caste and community than on the basis of class. In Indian society the fault lines between castes and communities are clearer and deeper than those between classes which are more vague and permeable and allow more or less easy passage across them to individuals and households. Moreover, those who speak for the rights of disadvantaged classes rarely belong to those classes themselves, whereas the leaders who demand more rights for the disadvantaged communities are often members of those communities. They are able to bring greater passion into their demands.

The demand, as a matter of right, for better representation in public life for the disadvantaged castes and communities has led to some changes in the social composition of the middle class. But it has also led to the deepening of the fault lines between castes and communities. Identity politics has no doubt led to a greater awareness of rights, but it has also led to the deepening of mistrust in public life.

* * *

The subject of trust is more difficult to deal with in a systematic way than that of rights if only because trust is often implicit whereas rights tend to be encoded in rules. When a right has been violated, one can always move the courts. But when trust has been abused, to whom should one turn?

Even while acknowledging fully the great importance of rights, it should be obvious that the legal or even the political machinery of the state cannot alone ensure that people are able to go about their daily tasks unhindered and unharmed. Most social transactions take place without any rights being invoked because people can take each other on trust, at least to some extent, even when they belong to diverse classes and communities, and, indeed, even when they are relative strangers to each other. It is difficult to exaggerate the importance of this kind of implicit trust in the operation of collective life. We are reminded of its importance from time to time when trust breaks down, and people have to take recourse to the law, or to politics, or to violence.

No institution can be sustained for long unless some of its members are prepared to act beyond the call of duty, at least some of the time. To do so is a moral rather than a legal obligation. Examples of such conduct can be found from the family, the school, or the hospital.

Such conduct can be explained only on the assumption that people are able to take each other on trust. It is not that the person who acts beyond the call of duty is unable to exercise his rights. But he is willing to keep those rights in abeyance, trusting that others too will some day act beyond the call of duty in the larger interest.

It is easiest to examine the social significance of trust and its interface with rights in the framework of particular institutions. I would like to begin with the study of the family which offers certain distinctive advantages for the purpose of this kind of enquiry. It is, besides, one of the oldest of social institutions, if not the oldest, and one that is present, in one form or another, in every human society.

The family may be found in many different forms in different societies and, even, in the same society. The nuclear family, with its simple structure of parents and unmarried children, is only one of the forms of the family. In India it co-exists with various other forms of it based on the extension, both lateral and vertical, of ties between close kin. The Indian family, whether simple or extended, operates within a broader universe in which relatives by both blood and marriage occupy different positions bearing different rights and obligations, even when they do not live in the same household. What distinguishes the Indian from the western system of kinship is the care with which relatives through the mother and the father are differentiated from each other, and each assigned a different function and a corresponding kinship term.

Within the domain of kinship, relatives are governed by what Meyer Fortes (1969: 219–49), the leading authority on the subject, has called 'the axiom of amity'. No doubt the axiom of amity does not operate with the same force between near and distant relatives. But it is expected to prevail between relatives who live in the same household or in adjacent ones. Within the family, whether in the narrow or the extended sense, relations are expected to be governed by reciprocity and, above all, trust. This does not mean that domestic life is simply a bed of roses. The same family which is expected to be governed by reciprocity and trust is also a hotbed of jealousy, suspicion, and mistrust.

Mutuality, reciprocity, and trust may be the bedrock of the family, but the family, like any other institution, cannot endure in the absence of a structure of rights. The simple point is that one does not have to invoke those rights at every turn in order to remain aware that one can fall back on them when there is a crisis. No institution can expect to endure without ever facing any crisis. But there is all the difference between coping with a crisis when it comes and inviting a crisis. Demanding the satisfaction of rights, in season and out of season, may be one way of inviting a crisis in an institution.

Anthropologists who have studied domestic institutions have pointed to the joint operation of legal and moral factors in their sustenance. Rights and obligations are as important as the axiom of amity, and they are no less important in simple tribal communities than in complex industrial societies. Rights may be defined by custom rather than statute. They are not only acknowledged but subject to adjudication even in communities with few material resources which subsist by hunting and gathering rather than agriculture or animal herding.

The traditional Hindu joint family was a legal entity (Shah 1998: 14–51). The distribution of rights within it was defined in part by law, but mainly by custom which often departed widely from the written code. Disputes arose about the use and disposal of joint-family property. The coparcenaries who were parties to the dispute might be brothers living together, or sons of co-resident brothers, or even a son and his father. A normal practice was to attribute responsibility for the disputes to the wives who were members of the household not by birth but by marriage. When disputes over who had the right over what reached a point of crisis, the joint family might be partitioned. There were established procedures to protect the rights of all the parties concerned at the time of partition (Madan 1989: 144–58).

The law, with its inevitable attention to rights, comes into play not only at the dissolution of the family but also at its creation. Its presence in the background as a guarantor of the rights of its members is not only desirable but also indispensable. How frequently and how actively it comes into the foreground is a question that must engage the attention of all serious students of domestic institutions, and of social institutions more generally.

Institutions change over time, partly in response to changes in their environment. This means that the distribution of rights within them as well as the balance between rights and trust also changes. If we look at the family in contemporary India, particularly the middle-class family, we will find that there has been a continuous process of the adjustment and readjustment of rights and responsibilities among its members. The family today is not what it was a hundred years ago, or even fifty years ago; yet it remains the basic workshop, so to say, of social reproduction.

One of the most significant social changes in our time has been the change in the position of women. This change has not affected all sections of Indian society equally. Its most manifest effect has been on the professional middle class in the metropolitan cities. University education and professional employment have given women a new sense of their rights and responsibilities. Education and employment require women to spend long hours outside the home and also give them a measure of financial independence. Their altered position in society necessarily brings about changes in their position in the household.

The family cannot survive as an institution if the acknowledged rights of some of its members are persistently and wilfully suppressed for the benefit of others. Of course there will be differences as to what those rights are and who is entitled to exactly what under them. The disputes that arise have to be resolved from one day to another, and they do get resolved where there is some minimum of trust within the household. A daily review of the rights of each member and a continuous exposure and analysis of their violation does not add to the wellbeing of either the family as a whole or its individual members.

When disagreements and disputes reach the point of no return, the family is partitioned or even dissolved. The break up of the family takes different forms in different societies. In some, disputes over property are pre-eminent, in others disputes over conjugal rights.

But one thing should be clear: the partition of an individual family or the dissolution of an individual marriage does not mean the end of domestic institutions, or the end of the rights and the trust on which such institutions must be based.

*　　*　　*

The family is no doubt the extreme example of a social institution for whose well-being the requirement of trust appears self-evident. But if my argument is valid, the same requirement has to be met, though, obviously, not in the same way, for the well-being of all institutions. It is not enough to guarantee that the rights of the members of a public institution such as a college, a hospital, or a bank be upheld; it is important also that trust obtains among those members.

As my second example, I will turn to academic institutions or institutions responsible for teaching and research. These vary greatly in their size of membership and their scale of operation. They include undergraduate colleges at one end and specialized centres for advanced scientific research at the other. Some are engaged mainly in teaching and do little or no research while others engage mainly in research and do little or no teaching. But they are all engaged, in one way or another, with the transmission of existing knowledge and the creation of new knowledge. An academic institution has a more distinct focus of activity than a domestic institution such as the family. Moreover, colleges, universities, and research institutes of the kind I have in mind are relatively new foundations whereas the family as an institution has existed since time immemorial.

My focus here will be not on the quality of work being done by individual scientists or scholars, but on the institutional setting in which that work is undertaken. It is often said that, while we have produced scientists and scholars of the first rank, our academic institutions, with a few exceptions, have failed to live up to the expectations with which they were established. Many of our most talented scientists and scholars are to be found overseas. Some of them say that they have been driven out of the country by the perennial disorder and inefficiency of our own institutions of science and scholarship.

It is a truism in the modern world that no scientist and no scholar can work entirely on his own. He needs support and sustenance from the work of other scientists and scholars. The organization of science and scholarship is undergoing major changes throughout the world. As I have pointed out elsewhere (Béteille 2009), individual scholars and scientists are turning increasingly to networks of interpersonal relations as supplements to the institutions in which they are employed. This kind of change is partly a response to the weakening of established institutions such as the universities, and this in turn leads to their further weakening.

The universities and colleges in India are beset with many problems today. There are many more of them than there were at the time of independence, but they have fallen in the public esteem and even in the esteem of their own thoughtful members. The regularity and routine of work is not maintained as before. This is not a failure of any particular individual but of the college or university as an institution.

Those who have to govern the universities complain about the paucity of their material resources. There is no doubt paucity of resources, but there is also wastage. It is true that our universities cannot provide the kind of facilities that the best of our scientists and scholars can command when they go abroad for work. But the problem of material resources is not the only one, nor, in my judgement, the principal one. In the 1920s and 1930s, scientists and scholars, such as C.V. Raman, Satyendra Nath Bose, and Suniti Kumar Chatterji at the University of Calcutta, did outstanding and ground-breaking work. Yet the material resources available to them were meagre. The deeper problem today is an institutional problem, or a problem of human relations.

If we want to hear the use of the language of rights in the full range and variety of its meanings, there is no better place to choose than the Indian university or college. The housewife may feel genuinely aggrieved that her rights are being disregarded or abused, but she can hardly articulate her grievance with the eloquence and emphasis, not to say vehemence, with which university teachers and even students speak about their rights.

If one spends any time in a university department, one is likely to hear from its head that the rights of his department are being disregarded by the vice-chancellor to the advantage of some other department headed, presumably, by a crony. One is likely to hear from junior members of the faculty that their rights in turn are being disregarded by the aggrieved head of department in the allocation of teaching duties or research funds, or both. Finally, no one can outdo the leaders of students' unions in their indignation at the violation of their rights by the authorities. Protests, demonstrations, and rallies by unions of students, teachers, and others provide regular opportunities for expanding and refining the vocabulary of rights.

I do not wish to belittle the importance of rights in the working of a college, or a university department, or of any other institution of teaching and research. Nor do I wish to make light of the need to defend those rights against persistent and wilful violation. Our universities and colleges which are designed to be open and secular institutions operate in a social environment in which the traditional demands of religion, caste, and community are still very strong. Apart from the divergence of interests among members that may be found in all institutions, there are deeper differences among members in the understanding and interpretation of the rights with which they are endowed or believe they are endowed. These differences of perception add substantially to the misunderstanding, mistrust, and suspicion among them.

It should be obvious that in any academic institution, whether a college, a post-graduate department, or a research institute, there has to be trust among individual members if what they undertake together is to achieve fruitful results. When students lose confidence in the capacity of their teachers to act without fear or favour, a great deal is lost on both sides. Effective teaching requires a close, even a personal, relationship between the student and his teacher, and such a relationship cannot be sustained solely through the definition and exercise of rights; it has to rest on mutual trust.

Successful teaching depends not just on technical ability but equally, if not more, on patience and care. It is a slow boring of hard boards. A teacher with only moderate technical ability may win the confidence of his students by imposing not his authority, but his goodwill on them, by acting in their interest beyond the call of duty. All of this becomes difficult when, for one reason or another, trust begins to falter and break down. It is true that there still remain individual teachers who will persevere even in the face of a deteriorating institutional environment, but sooner or later the deterioration in the environment begins to take its toll on individual effort.

One of the symptoms of the weakness and failure of trust is the reluctance to exercise academic judgement in the evaluation of students and colleagues. Yet academic work cannot advance without continuous scrutiny and review. The work of students needs to be evaluated. This cannot be done effectively and meaningfully by recourse only to 'objective' criteria and without the exercise of academic judgement for fear that if that judgement is adverse, it will be construed as having been made in bad faith. Many examiners are reluctant to turn down a PhD thesis because they do not want their good faith to be put in question; some examiners do, of course, fail students in order to spite the candidate or his supervisor. I sat for many years on a committee to review reports on PhD theses on which the examiners were divided. When it came to an adverse report, the inevitable response of the candidate's supervisor and the head of his department would be that the examiner was known to be a malicious and spiteful person. This left unexplained the fact that the examiner had been chosen, in almost every case, at the initiative of the supervisor and with the concurrence of the head of the department. Stories about malice, spite, and bad faith are told, retold, and embellished in academic institutions of every kind.

Science and scholarship cannot advance without a dependable and trustworthy system of peer review. Such a system has to enjoy the confidence of all concerned because he who is being reviewed today may be the reviewer tomorrow. I cannot judge how well peer review operates in the physical or the biological sciences. It does not operate effectively or meaningfully in the social sciences. Occasionally reviewers act spitefully; more commonly they provide reports that are equivocal, evasive, and vacuous.

*   *   *

When the first colleges and universities were established in India in the nineteenth century, they brought something new into the country, not just as centres of learning but also as social institutions. They were among the first open and secular institutions that were willing to accommodate members without consideration of caste and creed, and, before very long, also without consideration of gender. By the end of the nineteenth century they had established themselves as models for other public institutions and the nurseries in which they were conceived and designed.

The universities brought together persons from all castes and communities and enabled them to interact with each other on a more or less equal footing. This was a significant departure from the traditional order in which the hierarchical segregation of castes and communities was maintained in both town and village. Where there was closeness and not separation, as in the case of master and servant, or landowner and tenant, or patron and client, the closeness was governed by the rules of hierarchy, and not equality. Women too were admitted although they did not at first come in large numbers, and until the time of independence they were confined largely to colleges only for women.

In the nineteenth century and well into the twentieth, the universities and colleges were relatively small places. Although they were in principle open to all classes and communities, only some came to them, and they were not in any meaningful sense representative of India's vast and varied population. Not surprisingly, they became the preserves of the middle class rather than the working class or the peasantry. But the middle class itself had many gradations, and a gifted and talented student from a disadvantaged social background had the opportunity to make his mark in society if he managed to do well in the university.

Because they were relatively small and compact, the universities of the past give in hindsight an appearance of order and coherence that may in fact be deceptive. The British were certainly aware of the divisions of caste and community among both students and teachers, and they were not above playing on those divisions. But they were also wary of the turmoil that would follow if politics were given too free a hand. On the other side, the divisions of caste and community were kept in check, at least to some extent, by the demands of unity made by the nationalist movement to whose leadership graduates of the university contributed a substantial part. It was a point of honour within that movement to disregard considerations of caste and community in public life.

It is difficult to say today how far the universities of the past had succeeded in creating a basis of trust between teachers and students across the divisions of caste and community. Women students were few in number and women teachers fewer, except in women's colleges; in mixed institutions, women generally maintained a low profile. The idea that the minorities and the backward castes were not getting their due share in higher education had already begun to grow, but the colonial administration sought to address the problem by devising appropriate policies rather than creating new rights. The British were not in any case lavish in creating rights for their Indian subjects.

Things began to change with the coming of independence. A period of steady growth in the number and size of colleges and universities began and has continued until the present day. The increase in number and size has been accompanied by changes in the social composition and the political temperature of the universities. Indeed it can be argued that the expansion of higher education in India has been driven more by social and political compulsions than by academic considerations.

There has been unremitting pressure on the colleges and universities to admit more students and appoint more teachers. A university degree is indispensable for employment in middle-class occupations, and that accounts for a great deal of the pressure for admissions. Large and increasing numbers of students enter a college or even a post-graduate department not in search of new knowledge but in order to secure a degree. Perhaps this was the case to a certain extent even before independence, but today acquiring new knowledge and securing a university degree have become de-linked from each other openly and without pretence or embarrassment. For many, perhaps most, of those who seek admission to them, colleges and universities are not so much centres of learning or even social institutions as necessary conduits in the process of career advancement.

Pressures for admission and promotion notwithstanding, attendance in colleges and universities is often thin. Even those who are registered as full-time students often engage in other pursuits outside the college or university. There are not only absentee students but absentee lecturers and professors as well. The close interchange between students and teachers which provides the basis for the college or the university as an academic institution is no longer the general pattern. Teachers are obliged to relax their grip over attendance and the other requirements of membership, and they learn easily to take their own institutional obligations lightly. Students who meet the basic formal requirements of attendance and examination can generally count on getting their degrees because everybody knows that too high a rate of failure will not be politically acceptable.

With the growth in number and size, the social composition of the colleges and universities has changed. Socially, both students and teachers are more diverse, not to say heterogeneous, than they were at the beginning of the twentieth century. They now come from a wider range of castes and communities than before. The middle class has become more differentiated and more stratified over time, and individuals from its various layers and strata may be found in the universities, though not in equal proportions. Many manual workers in the organized sector, particularly in large public sector undertakings, are able to send their children to good secondary schools from where they are able to move easily into colleges and universities, but children of workers in the vast unorganized sector remain largely outside them. My sense is that the social composition of the Indian university has become more mixed in terms of caste and community than in terms of class.

Greater diversity in the social composition of academic institutions would have come about through the natural process of their growth and expansion. But in India a large part in this has been played by active political intervention. This political intervention has been more mindful of the disparities among castes and communities than of those between social classes. The leaders of disadvantaged castes and communities claim better representation in academic institutions for their members as a matter of right, and these claims receive sympathetic attention from legislators and even judges. Heads of premier academic institutions are put on the defensive when they are asked to explain why there are so few members of the backward castes and the minorities in their institutions. They know that this may be because few of them are able to withstand the tough competition for admission, but they are made to feel that they may be violating some important right.

There is no reason to believe that diversity as such must lead to the failure of trust. What is leading to the failure of trust today is not diversity as such but the kind of identity politics that uses that diversity as a prop for claiming special rights for disadvantaged castes and communities. These special rights cannot but come into collision with the equal rights that all individuals feel they can claim as citizens.

The language of rights is used again and again to trump any argument about the need to uphold academic standards in admissions, appointments, and promotions. The determination of the government to make the colleges and universities socially inclusive has had the consequence of making them very uneven in terms of the academic competence of both students and teachers. Those in them who are seriously committed to science and scholarship complain, with some justification, that academic standards have been lowered.

The lowering of academic standards is not the only matter for concern. What should be a matter of as much concern is the widespread suspicion and mistrust prevalent in academic institutions in the country today. Perhaps the mistrust was always present below the surface. But it is now out in the open and being given new strength and legitimacy by the language of rights.

Let me repeat in conclusion the fundamental importance of a framework of rights in the operation of any institution. Every member of a university or an institute of advanced study and research has the right to treatment as an equal, if not the right to equal treatment. That right is not negotiable. But that very right comes into jeopardy when trust between members falls to a low ebb.

References

Ali, Ayaan Hirsi. 2007. *Infidel.* London: Pocket Books.

Béteille, André. 2000a. *Antinomies of Society.* New Delhi: Oxford University Press.

————. 2000b. 'Anarchy and the Abuse of Power', *Economic and Political Weekly*, vol. xxxv, no. 10, pp. 779–83.

————. 2005. 'Matters of Right and of Policy', *Seminar*, no. 549, pp. 17–21.

————. 2009. 'Institutions and Networks', *Current Science*, vol. 97, no. 2, pp. 148–56.

Bose, N.K. (ed.). 1962. *Studies in Gandhism.* Calcutta: Merit Publishers.

Chaudhuri, Nirad C. 1951. *The Autobiography of an Unknown Indian.* London: Macmillan.

Dworkin, Ronald. 1984. *Taking Rights Seriously.* London: Duckworth.

Erikson, R. and J.H. Goldthorpe. 1992. *The Constant Flux.* Oxford: Clarendon Press.

Fortes, Meyer. 1969. *Kinship and the Social Order.* London: Routledge & Kegan Paul.

Gandhi, M.K. 1962. *Village Swaraj.* Ahmedabad: Navjivan Publishing House.

Madan, T.N. 1989. *Family and Kinship.* New Delhi: Oxford University Press.

Marshall, T.H. 1977. *Class, Citizenship and Social Development.* Chicago: University of Chicago Press.

Shah, A.M. 1998. *The Family in India.* New Delhi: Orient Longman.

6

Caste and the Citizen*

I will discuss here the distinctive features of Indian society and the ways in which those features may be represented. The first is the representation of India as a society of castes and communities, and the second as a nation of citizens. Each representation corresponds to significant aspects of the past and present reality, the first to an order sanctioned by immemorial tradition and the second to an order expressing the aspirations of India's political leaders at the time of independence.

The systematic study of human societies began with the recognition that each society has a distinct morphological structure and that different societies have different structures. In their early phase of enquiry and analysis, sociologists and social anthropologists were inclined to use the organic analogy widely and somewhat loosely. In the nineteenth century, the organic analogy was used extensively by the great English sociologist Herbert Spencer. It was also used widely in France by August Comte who was Spencer's senior contemporary and by Émile Durkheim who was his junior contemporary and the leading French sociologist of the late nineteenth and early twentieth century. Durkheim (1964) used the organic analogy to construct a

* This chapter was previously published in *Science and Culture*, vol. 77, nos 3–4, 2011, pp. 83–90.

typology of human societies or, at least, to formulate rules for the classification of social types.

Social anthropologist A.R. Radcliffe-Brown, who was Durkheim's follower in Britain, extended the use of the analogy. Apart from the analogy between the individual organism and the structure of a society, Radcliffe-Brown (1957) noted that certain animal species, particularly among insects, are governed by a kind of division of labour from which something might be learnt about the organization of social life among human beings. Radcliffe-Brown realized of course that the analogy between humans and other animals could at best be used as a starting point for the study of human societies and that the organic analogy had to be used with great caution in view of the complexity, the fluidity, and the dynamism of human society and culture.

While sociologists in general seek to identify structures or patterns in collective life and to study them systematically and comparatively, they do not all favour the use of the organic analogy. The opponents of that analogy would say that in studying animals we study behaviour whereas in studying human beings we study meaningful action. If ants and bees assign meanings to their conduct, we cannot find out what those meanings are whereas meanings are important components of human action.

In dealing with human social arrangements, as against social arrangements among other animals, we have to deal with what Edward Shils (1982: 275–383) has called the 'self-contemplation of society'. Human beings everywhere carry an image or a map of their own society and often of other societies as well. Such a social map is not always coherent and is rarely free from inconsistencies, not to say contradictions. As societies grow larger and more complex, the 'self-contemplation of society' becomes more clearly articulated. This happens partly through the emergence of intellectual specialists whose task it is to rationalize, systematize, and articulate society's consciousness of itself. It gives rise at the same time to divergent representations of the same society and to disputes regarding their respective merits.

It is unlikely that all individuals carry the same map of the society of which they are members. As a society expands in scale and becomes more differentiated, the images and representations become more diverse. Men and women, privileged and disadvantaged classes, and members of different religious communities are likely to view from somewhat different angles the same society of which they are all members. With the passage of time the divisions and subdivisions in a society change. Old divisions become effaced and new ones emerge. With these changes in the contours of society, the ways in which people view their society also undergo change. Despite all the variation and change, certain representations become established over time and acquire a kind of objective presence. These may be called the dominant representations of a society, and it is on these dominant representations that I will focus my attention.

*   *   *

I now turn to a discussion of two representations of society that vie with each other for pre-eminence in contemporary India. The first is the representation of India as a society of castes and communities, and the second its representation as a nation of citizens. The first has its roots in immemorial tradition and derives its legitimacy from it. The second is of more recent provenance and derives its legitimacy from the Constitution of India and the political ideals that gave shape to it.

The traditional social order had a hierarchical design. It was based on the primacy of kinship, caste, and community, and the individual as a citizen had only a small place in it. While a great deal of diversity of customs and practices between the castes and communities was tolerated or even encouraged, the individual was bound by the customs and practices of the group of which he was a member by birth. Many commentators, including Nehru (1961), had pointed out that it was the group and not the individual that counted in the traditional social order. The individual could of course follow his own inner voice and renounce the world in order to become a wandering mendicant or a *sannyasi*. But there is a world of difference between the individual as sannyasi and the individual as citizen.

British rule initiated a process of churning in life and thought in nineteenth-century India. It opened up the prospect and the possibility of a new kind of social order that would be quite different from what had prevailed for centuries. By the end of the nineteenth century reflective Indians began to take an increasing interest in the ideas of citizenship, nationhood, and democracy which the British brought with them as a part of their intellectual capital to India. The British themselves were not always happy when they thought of the political uses to which their Indian subjects might put the ideas to which they were being increasingly exposed. Their view by and large was that the Indians were subjects and not citizens and that they should be kept content in their subjecthood. But the genie had been released from the bottle, and it was not going to be easy to put it back there again.

New institutions, associations, and professions began to emerge and to extend their influence in the country. Again, these were often established at the initiative of the British, but Indians soon began to make themselves at home in them, and sometimes to wrest the initiative in their establishment and maintenance from their colonial masters. The universities, the legal and medical professions, the civic bodies, and, after 1885, the Congress party provided Indians with the kind of experience that would enable them before long to give shape and substance to the ideals of citizenship and nationhood.

The part played by open and secular institutions in the process of nation-building cannot be too strongly emphasized. The first modern universities in India were set up in 1857 in Calcutta, Bombay, and Madras. They were from the start open and secular institutions which brought together persons belonging to different castes and communities and established new social practices and relationships (Béteille 2010). They also enabled men and women to interact with each other and created a new sense of the possibilities of individual achievement. Whereas in the West, and particularly in England, the universities had lagged behind in the movement from hierarchy to equality, in India they were in the forefront of that movement. They, along with their colleges, became the workshops in which ideas for a new kind of social order were forged and tested.

The new professions too played a part in developing the ideals of citizenship and nationhood. Indians entered the law colleges established in Calcutta, Bombay, Madras, and elsewhere, and some of them went to London for further qualification. They joined the bar and the bench in India where they worked alongside English lawyers and judges. It is remarkable how quickly they mastered the principles of the new jurisprudence. They soon learned through hard experience that if they were to claim parity with English lawyers and judges, they would have to concede parity to their fellow Indians without consideration of caste and community.

It is remarkable how many lawyers—Gandhi, Nehru, and Patel, to name only the most eminent—joined the nationalist movement and took charge of its leadership. It is equally remarkable how many of them, notably B.R. Ambedkar, became members of the Constituent Assembly and gave shape to India's republican Constitution. Their commitment to freedom from colonial rule made it inevitable for them to favour the image of India as a nation of citizens as against a society of castes and communities.

The divisions of caste and community did not disappear simply because the leaders of the nationalist movement were uneasy about those divisions which many of them regarded as obstacles to nationhood and citizenship. They remain as important features of the social landscape of India to this day. Some of the energy that was invested in the process of nation-building before independence became gradually dissipated after independence. Politics took many unforeseen turns, and large numbers of people have become inured to the politics of caste and community even when they feel uneasy about them. It is this ambivalence about what kind of society India is and ought to be that gives to Indian democracy a character of its own.

* * *

As the British settled down to the administration of India, they undertook to survey the land and its people methodically and systematically. Settlement and survey became important components of colonial rule by the middle of the nineteenth century. The British had entered a new and unfamiliar social world, and their curiosity was aroused by it. But they also had to bring the land and its people under their grasp in the interest of firm and effective administration.

From the middle of the nineteenth century onwards, after the administration of the country came directly under the crown, a new breed of civil servants began to arrive in India. Many of the young men who came—there were no women—had been educated in the best universities in Britain, and some of them had a genuine interest in science and scholarship and aspired to make their own contribution to knowledge. No doubt they came out to rule, but they also came to observe, record, describe, analyse, and even construct theories about the new world they had come to inhabit. We will fail to make a just assessment of the vast body of work they produced if we ignore the intellectual ambitions of the men who ruled India.

The English intellectual tradition, in which the new breed of civil servants was reared, had a marked empiricist bias. The observation and description of facts had the pride of place in it. Throughout the nineteenth century and well into the twentieth, the British were the best ethnographers in the world. No doubt they were helped by the fact that they also had a vast and far-flung empire. But the ethnography itself cannot be treated simply as an instrument of imperial policy.

The Indian intellectual tradition was very different in its orientation and, in any case, it had remained relatively stagnant for a long time. Its bias was for formal disciplines such as mathematics, grammar, logic, and metaphysics, and not empirical ones such as history, geography, and ethnography. The new science of ethnography was brought into India by the British. It is doubtful that Indians would on their own have created such a science for themselves in the nineteenth century.

The civil servants were not the sole creators of the ethnography of India. Missionaries, and even explorers and travellers, contributed something to its creation. The encouragement and support of the government enabled the ethnographic surveys to be organized on a scale that no private scholar could match. Indian assistants were used from the start, and from the beginning of the twentieth century they were publishing ethnographic accounts jointly with their British seniors, and then independently. Soon Indian ethnographers were making their own contributions to the study of tribal and other communities. The first post-graduate department of anthropology was started in the University of Calcutta in 1920, and the first professional journal, *Man in India*, was established in 1921 under the editorship of the doyen of Indian ethnography, S.C. Roy, and with financial support from the colonial government.

The decennial census was harnessed for listing all individuals according to tribe, caste, sect, religion, and language. This was an ambitious exercise which sought to pigeonhole individuals into categories that were not always clear-cut or well-defined. But the enumeration of caste as a part of the census had become an established practice by 1931. The Commissioner for the census of 1931 was J.H. Hutton, then a member of the Indian Civil Service (ICS) and soon to become the William Wyse Professor of Anthropology in the University of Cambridge. Hutton's report gives some idea of the pitfalls associated with the enumeration of castes to the satisfaction of all concerned (Hutton 1961: Appendix A).

The census did not stop with the listing of castes and communities. The broader objective was to use the materials provided by the census to create a comprehensive social map of the people of India. This was a difficult and ambitious objective, particularly in view of the fact that a system which had always had its ambiguities had entered a significant phase of change. The lists provided a large and bewildering variety of names. Sometimes the same community might use different names in different locations, and sometimes the same name might be appropriated by different and unrelated communities. The first task, therefore, was to create order in the confusion of names by adopting some kind of reasonable classification. The classifications adopted were never free from major deficiencies.

The classification of the innumerable communities encountered by the census takers proved to be no easy task. The ethnographers were often misled by an excess of zeal to overlook the snares and pitfalls that lay on their way. They knew that in principle a tribe was different from a caste, but when it came to labelling a particular community, they could not avoid inconsistency so that the same group was sometimes called a caste and sometimes a tribe. The vast size of the country and the diversity of its population made the task of producing a single and uniform classification of communities for India as a whole a difficult and frustrating exercise.

Attempts at the classification of castes were accompanied by attempts at their ranking. Census commissioners such as H.H. Risley and J.H. Hutton sought to construct theories of the origins of caste. Some maintained that its roots lay in religion, and others that it was rooted in the peculiar rules of kinship and marriage. In this process they developed the argument that the key to the structure of Hindu society lay in the structure of caste. Their fascination with the classification and ranking of castes led many of them to believe that there was something immutable and indestructible in the system.

The actual ranking of castes was never as rigid or inflexible as the schemes devised by the census authorities presumed. Once the process of drawing up a ranking of castes began, claims and counterclaims began to be presented to the authorities on behalf of a variety of castes. Their leaders often argued that the authorities had assigned ranks to them that did not do justice to their current or their traditional social standing. No doubt the authorities took some pleasure in being sought out as arbiters in such delicate and yet vital matters relating to social distinction. They felt that they could act both knowledgeably and impartially. Their confidence in the importance of their work became reinforced.

The ranking of castes became an obsession with many ethnographers. They were often misled by their own theoretical preconceptions. They failed by and large to see the fundamental distinction between caste as *varna* and caste as *jati*, treating the latter as simple subdivisions of the former. Varna represents a conceptual scheme, the 'thought-out' order, so to say, as against the 'lived-in' reality of jati. Because the varnas could be arranged in a simple linear order of ranks from the highest to the lowest, they believed that, with time and patience, they would be able to arrange all the jatis in such an order of ranks. This was a delusion which merely intensified the competition for claims of superior rank and, with it, the consciousness of caste.

The hierarchy of caste was no doubt more rigid than the social hierarchy in Britain and elsewhere in the West in the middle of the nineteenth century. It is understandable that the British ethnographers exaggerated the rigidity of caste hierarchy when they first came face to face with it. It is ironical nevertheless that a growing section of the Indian intelligentsia was soon to adopt a critical attitude towards the hierarchy of caste which they saw as antithetical to the democratic ideals of equality and liberty to which they were being increasingly attracted.

The divisions and rivalries between castes, brought to the fore by the continuing preoccupation with their classification and ranking, had political implications that did not remain hidden for long. As Indians became more aware of the British interest in caste, many caste leaders approached the authorities and said that their community had been unjustly treated by society and that the government should do something to ensure that their just interests were protected and promoted. The British were not above playing one community against another and thus securing their own hold over the country through a policy of 'divide and rule'.

These various moves and countermoves have led to what Louis Dumont (1966: 280) has called the 'substantialization of caste'. In other words, each caste became conscious of its distinctive identity and different castes began to compete with each other for status and, even more, for power.

The enlarged role of caste in the political process was viewed with increasing misgiving by the leaders of the nationalist movement. What they wanted above all was to leave the divisions of caste and community behind and to lead the country into a new future which would be governed by the principles of liberal democracy. Both sides believed that caste and democracy were incompatible. The nationalists believed that they could break free from the fetters of caste by which Indian society had been held back for centuries. The British were on the whole sceptical even when they made increasing room for democratic practices and institutions.

*   *   *

Some of the policies and actions of the colonial government served to give a new lease of life to caste. Whether they were intended to do so or not is a different matter, but that was sometimes their consequence. There were other policies and actions, however, which had the opposite effect and served to undermine the social order based on caste. We must not condemn the British for doing things that reinforced caste and withhold credit from them for releasing forces that not only weakened the existing social order but brought into view the prospect of a new kind of society.

British rule introduced new ideas and institutions and also laid the foundations of a new middle class based on education and occupation. This middle class was still relatively small when the country became independent in 1947, but it has grown significantly in size since then. Its growth required some relaxation of the restrictions of caste, but its members have not always been shy to use the resources of caste to promote their own interests even against their proclaimed ideals and values.

The modernization of Indian society witnessed the emergence from the middle of the nineteenth century onwards of a variety of open and secular institutions such as schools, colleges, banks, law courts, and civic bodies that were different in their composition and character from the traditional institutions based on kinship, caste, and community. They were open in the sense that membership in them could be acquired, at least in principle, without consideration of birth, and they were secular in the sense that they were not regulated by religious rules or religious authorities. These institutions were sponsored initially by the British, but Indians soon began to take a large part in their operation and management. The new institutions gave increasing scope to individual initiative and ambition, and became, in course of time, workshops for the training in citizenship.

Even while the colonial ethnographers were elaborating and refining their representation of Indian society as an inflexible and immutable order of castes and communities, that society was beginning to change. We must not exaggerate the extent and scope of the change, but we cannot deny that it was taking place and slowly undermining, if not the operation of caste, at least its legitimacy. Even Mahatma Gandhi, who had begun as a champion of *varnashramadharma*, had to tone down and then abandon his defence of caste.

Even while the ethnographers were continuing to accumulate evidence of caste customs and practices, many progressive Indians had begun to believe, somewhat optimistically, that caste was on its way out. The evidence, as we look back, appears somewhat mixed. There is evidence of the weakening of caste as well as of its increasing strength.

I would like to begin with the ritual opposition of purity and pollution which, when ethnographic studies began in the middle of the nineteenth century, was a central feature of the social order of caste. Some of the ethnographers of that time were acquainted with the classical literature of India including the *Dharmashastra*. They were struck by the correspondence between what they read in the texts and what they saw in the field, although the correspondence was far from perfect. It was, however, close enough, at least in their view, to lead them to believe that they were in the face of a unique social world that had remained unchanged for centuries if not millennia.

The ritual rules that received the most attention in the ethnographic literature were those relating to the exchange of food and water. The rules were not only very stringent, they were also very elaborate. Restrictions on the acceptance of food were indicative of the separation as well as the hierarchy of castes. Castes of equal or roughly equal rank accepted food from each other. Superior castes gave cooked food to inferior ones but did not accept it from them. Restrictions did not stop with food but applied also to the acceptance of water. Not everyone could offer drinking water to members of the superior castes. In many parts of the country the superior castes denied access to their wells to the lowest castes, causing considerable privation and hardship to them.

Ritual restrictions on the interchange of food and water have weakened all around and the decline appears to be irreversible. Many of the practices observed two or three generations ago have not only become obsolete, but now appear anachronistic and some seem hardly credible. If caste was mainly a matter of ritual then there was good reason for believing at the time of independence that the system had been discredited and was on its way out. Indians who were working for freedom from colonial rule did not wish to be reminded of the peculiar practices of their forefathers.

Traditional economic activities had been so organized in the past as to be able to accommodate the ritual practices of caste without too much strain. The cycle of agricultural activities and the annual ritual cycle had become adjusted with each other through long usage. The new institutions and organizations that began to emerge from the middle of the nineteenth century established routines of work that were quite different from those of the past. It became increasingly difficult to undertake elaborate daily rituals without disrupting work in the new institutional setting. Adjustments were no doubt made at first, as a result of which both the work and the ritual suffered. In course of time, the ritual practices came to be squeezed out as the new open and secular institutions gained ground.

A close association between caste and occupation had played an important part in the maintenance of caste identities. In the past the caste system provided the social basis for an elaborate division of labour in the economy of land and grain. Each caste, and sometimes each subcaste, was, at least in principle, associated with a certain occupation which was regarded as the traditional occupation of its members even though they might not all actually practice it.

The association between caste and occupation was never rigid, although the principle on which it was based was widely acknowledged. Today the principle itself is disregarded and even rejected. A new occupational system has gradually displaced the old one, and this is one of the most significant changes taking place in India today. Particularly in the more dynamic sectors of the economy there is a predominance of what may be called 'caste-free occupations'. There is no caste or subcaste that has any special claims on occupations such as software engineer or management consultant as there were for those of the potter or the barber.

With the gradual, and it would appear inevitable, displacement of the old occupational system by a new one, the loyalty to traditional crafts and services has become weakened. In the past a person took pride in his ancestral occupation, no matter how lowly it was, and hoped to prepare his offspring for induction in it. This is no longer the case. Even temple priests now want their sons to learn English and hope they will become engineers, or managers, or civil servants.

Pride in the ancestral craft has been undermined by the aspiration for occupational mobility. It is not that there was no mobility in the past, but mobility in the caste system which has been studied extensively by sociologists (Srinivas 1968) was significantly different from occupational mobility in an expanding economy. Caste mobility took place in slow motion, as it were, whereas occupational mobility is rapid in its pace. But there is a more important difference. The unit of mobility in the old system was the group—a subcaste or a group of lineages—whereas the unit of mobility in the new system is the individual or the household.

The inevitable consequence of increasing individual mobility is that it leads to the differentiation of each caste and even subcaste in terms of income, occupation, and education. Even in the past there might be internal differentiation within the caste, but the nature of mobility was such that it led the caste to be split in the long run into two or more subcastes. This does not happen under conditions of rapid individual mobility, and the caste simply becomes internally more and more differentiated without the formation of new subcastes as in the past. Paradoxically this continues to happen even as the leaders of the caste strive to give its members a keener sense of their own political identity.

As individual mobility increases with the expansion of the middle class, the individual finds it increasingly difficult to carry his caste or even his extended kin group along with him as he moves from one social level to another. Differences of income, occupation, and education become more important in social life than the distinctions of caste, at least at the upper levels of the middle class in metropolitan cities. The old rules of marriage become relaxed, at least to some extent. Even where caste remains a consideration in marriage, it is the family rather than the subcaste that takes over the responsibility for the regulation of marriage. There are sensational reports in the press about the role of *khap panchayats* in the regulation of marriage in some rural areas, but such panchayats are becoming an anachronism.

In ritual matters, in the choice of occupations, and in matrimonial arrangements the role of caste has weakened progressively. It has weakened but not disappeared. Caste is not just a matter of social arrangement, it is also a matter of consciousness. The consciousness of caste as a basis for social identity remains even among people whose lives are no longer strictly regulated by the rules of caste. Similarly, the consciousness of membership in a particular religious community might remain very acute among persons who do not abide by any of the beliefs and practices prescribed by that religion.

There is an ebb and flow in the consciousness of caste and community that does not follow exactly the same pattern as changes in education and employment. While the evidence points to the decline of caste in many fields of economic and social life, there is one domain, that of politics, in which caste has increased its hold. It would not be too much to say that democratic politics has given a new lease of life to caste. It is this, no less than poverty and economic inequality, that challenges the prospect of making India into a nation of citizens.

* * *

India stood at the crossroads when independence came to the country in 1947. It was a time of great expectation and euphoria. The mood of the time was nicely captured by Nehru's 'tryst with destiny speech' in which he had said, 'A moment comes, which comes but rarely in history, when we step out from the old to the new, when an age ends, and when the soul of a nation, long suppressed, finds utterance' (Mukherjee 2007: 185). This sense that they were making history gave to India's leaders at that time the confidence and the determination to rise to the challenge of creating a new nation of free and equal citizens unconstrained by the ties of caste and community.

It can hardly be denied that the leaders of the nation at that time were men of exceptional ability and imagination. They had gone through a long and arduous struggle in which they had been sustained by the vision of a new life for their people. Did they forget all about the obstacles that lay in their way?

There were pragmatists as well as visionaries among the early leaders of independent India. They could not write a new constitution without keeping practical considerations in mind. Moreover, independence had been preceded by the trauma of partition, and some of them had experienced the force of the non-Brahmin movement in peninsular India. As such, they were not blind to the challenges that the resurgence of caste and community could pose to the process of nation-building in independent India.

The anxiety that troubled some of the leaders even at that time was well expressed in the Constituent Assembly by Govind Ballabh Pant, a prominent member of the Congress party, later to become the home minister of India. He had said:

> The individual citizen who is really the backbone of the State … has been lost here in that indiscriminate body known as the community. We have even forgotten that a citizen exists as such. There is the unwholesome, and to some extent a degrading habit of thinking always in terms of communities and never in terms of citizens. (*CAD* 1989, I–VI: 332)

Pant was cheered as he spoke but that did not mean that people were going to give up thinking in terms of communities and to think only in terms of citizens.

The same spirit was expressed only a few years later by Kaka Kalelkar, the chairman of the first Backward Classes Commission, in the letter he wrote to the President of India while forwarding the report of his commission to him. His letter went against the majority recommendation to introduce caste-based quotas in employment. In it he maintained that the individual and the nation should stand above everything else and that 'nothing should be allowed to organize itself between these two ends to the detriment of the freedom of the individual and the solidarity of the nation' (GoI 1956: iv).

The confidence of people like Nehru in the prospects for India as a nation of citizens was sustained by the convenient belief that the fractious divisions of caste and community had been fostered if not created by the British. As always the realist who did not hesitate to speak his mind, Dr Ambedkar took pains to remind the members of the Constituent Assembly of the responsibilities they would have to shoulder in order to make the new constitution work. He said in his closing speech to the Assembly, 'But let us not forget that this independence has thrown on us great responsibilities. By independence we have lost the excuse of blaming the British for anything going wrong. If hereafter things go wrong, we will have nobody to blame except ourselves' (*CAD* 1989, XII: 980).

More than sixty years have elapsed since the country became independent, but the jury is still out on whether we will become a nation of citizens or remain a society of castes and communities. With the advantage of hindsight one can see that it would have been impossible to exclude altogether the operation of caste in the political arena. But the extent to which it has penetrated that arena and become a consideration in all political calculations is unsettling. The British had their own reasons for using caste in their political manoeuvres. But the sustained and relentless use for political gains made by today's leaders makes those manoeuvres look like the work of amateurs.

I believe that Indians have become inured to the fact that their political leaders today are of a lesser breed than the ones who brought freedom to the country and created its republican constitution. They no longer look to their politicians for the regeneration of Indian society. It was perhaps natural to look to the politicians for the regeneration of India at the time of independence. But there is no reason to assume that the failure of the political leadership at a certain turn in the country's history must stand for the failure of the country as a whole.

When a country with a population as large and diverse as India's begins to change, its different sectors do not all change at the same pace or even in the same direction. It is worth noting that while politics and governance became increasingly fractious and ineffective in the last two decades, the same period witnessed steady and commendable advances in the economy. The economy is now no longer tied down to what used to be called 'the Hindu rate of growth'. The Indian economy is beginning to be regarded as a powerhouse all over the world. A considerable amount of initiative and energy is now also invested in voluntary associations which operate in the social sector which is distinct from both government and business.

Science, technology, business, enterprise, and voluntary action draw individuals into fields of activity in which the claims of caste and community, on which our vote banks thrive, cannot be easily accommodated. As he enters into new relationships in all these fields, the individual becomes increasingly aware of his rights as a citizen. But the awareness of rights does not create automatically or at once the awareness of responsibilities. Yet the individual becomes a citizen in the full sense only when the obligations of citizenship become ingrained in him in the way in which obligations to caste and community were ingrained in earlier generations of people.

Citizenship is not just a matter of rights, it is also a matter of attitudes and values. Those attitudes take time to become established in the hearts and minds of people. Nothing is easier than to inscribe new rights in a constitution, and nothing more difficult than to change the habits of the heart.

The habits of citizenship are not a gift of nature; they are a product of history. They grow and mature slowly, under particular social and political conditions. We must not assume that those conditions are present everywhere and at all times. In India today some of the prevalent conditions are favourable to the growth of citizenship while others are adverse. We must not focus our attention on only those conditions that favour its growth and take our eyes away from the ones that hinder it.

The Indian social tradition, as I have already said, favoured the group over the individual. This was true to some extent of all pre-modern societies, but it was particularly true of India. The citizen is, above all, an individual, and his rights and responsibilities exist without consideration of his membership of any caste or community. An individual may not belong to any caste or community but still be a citizen, whereas until 1850, at least among the Hindus, expulsion from caste amounted to civil death.

Even in Britain, where the institutions of constitutional democracy became established early, the advance of citizenship from the eighteenth to the twentieth century and beyond was a slow and uneven process (Marshall 1977). In India, the roadblocks against the advance of citizenship are more numerous and more obdurate. Both government and opposition have in the last few decades used these roadblocks for their own political gains instead of attempting to clear them. For this reason the future remains uncertain. What is certain is that we can no longer depend solely or even mainly on our political leadership to clear the way for building a nation of citizens. We were exceptionally lucky in the political leaders we had at the time of independence: Gandhi, Nehru, Ambedkar, and many others. It was a mistake to have thought that our luck would last for ever. It has now run out, and we have to look beyond our fractious and self-serving political leadership if the endeavour to build a nation of citizens that was begun at the time of independence is to continue and advance.

References

Béteille, André. 2010. *Universities at the Crossroads*. New Delhi: Oxford University Press.

Constituent Assembly Debates (CAD). 1989. *Official Report*. New Delhi: Government of India, vols I–XII.

Dumont, Louis. 1966. *Homo hierarchicus*. Paris: Gallimard.

Durkheim, Émile. 1964. *The Rules of Sociological Method*. New York: Free Press.

Hutton, J.H. 1961. *Caste in India*. New Delhi: Oxford University Press.

Government of India (GoI). 1956. *Report of the Backward Classes Commission 1955*. New Delhi (Chairman: Kaka Kalelkar).

Marshall, T.H. 1977. *Class, Citizenship and Social Development*. Chicago: University of Chicago Press.

Mukherjee, Rudrangshu (ed.). 2007. *Great Speeches of Modern India*. New Delhi: Random House.

Nehru, Jawaharlal. 1961. *The Discovery of India*. Bombay: Asia Publishing House.

Radcliffe-Brown, A.R. 1957. *A Natural Science of Society*. Glencoe: Free Press.

Shils, Edward. 1982. *The Constitution of Society*. Chicago: University of Chicago Press.

Srinivas, M.N. 1968. 'Mobility in the Caste System', in Milton Singer and Bernard S. Cohn (eds), *Structure and Change in Indian Society*. Chicago: Aldine, pp. 189–200.

7

Pluralism and Liberalism

The Indian social tradition is a pluralist tradition; it is not a liberal one. In making such a statement I am not unmindful of the hazard of attaching a single label to such a fluid and amorphous phenomenon as a social tradition, particularly in the case of India whose traditions are replete with so many divergent, not to say contradictory, aims and tendencies. It is nevertheless possible to identify certain persistent modes of thought and action that have withstood the many changes that have taken place in the country in its passage from the middle of the nineteenth century to the beginning of the twenty-first.

My aim here is not simply to explain what is happening in Indian society today but also to examine a little more closely the meanings of two terms that are widely used in public debate and discussion. The terms 'pluralist' and 'liberal' are widely, not to say promiscuously, used to characterize Indian society in the past as well as the present. But I will argue that, although their meanings overlap to some extent, there are also important differences in their connotations. It is on the differences that I will focus the main part of my attention.

It has often been pointed out by observers from both within the country and outside that Indian society accommodated diversity of customs and practices to a remarkable extent. The accommodation extended to the acceptance of not only a plurality of legal codes but also a plurality of religious creeds. This has sometimes been attributed to the polytheistic spirit of Hinduism which, unlike monotheistic religions such as Judaism, Christianity, and Islam, did not demand strict obedience to a single god or strict adherence to a single faith. The Christian missionaries of the nineteenth century regarded this as a moral failing, but others who have been appalled by the ferocity of ideological conflicts in the twentieth century and beyond might regard it as a moral advantage.

While tolerance of diversity can and generally does contribute something to the sustenance of the liberal outlook, it is not by itself sufficient to constitute a liberal social and political order. A general tolerance of diversity might sometimes lead, as it has done in the past, to the tolerance of highly illiberal practices. All kinds of practices, such as the subjugation of women, polygamy, and child marriage, have been allowed to continue on the ground that if a particular community or section of society has adhered to them since time immemorial and values them for that reason even today, the tolerance of diversity requires that the wider society should not seek to put any restraint on them. This kind of argument is not infrequently made in the defence of what has come to be known as 'multi-culturalism'.

The tolerance of diversity is certainly an important component of the liberal outlook, but it is not its only component and perhaps not even its most important one. An indispensable component of a liberal social and political order is respect for the autonomy of the individual and his freedom to choose his own life for himself and to live it in a fruitful, honourable, and dignified way. In practice, of course, there are all kinds of restraints on this in every society. The test of a liberal society lies in the extent to which it seeks to ease those restraints and to enlarge the capacity of the individual to live his own life according to his own tastes and preferences.

It is not enough to point to the tolerance of diversity in India's traditional social order. One must go a little further and ask how this diversity was organized. The simple answer, which needs consideration in some detail, is that it was organized hierarchically and not democratically. This was not unique to Indian society. Many past societies were in fact organized hierarchically, but the social hierarchy in India was more elaborate, more rigid, and more long-lasting than in any society known to human history. Its marks may still be seen in virtually every sphere of Indian society in the twenty-first century.

A hierarchical society, no matter how tolerant of diversity, acts against liberal institutions in two important ways. First, it tolerates inequalities of a kind with which no liberal order can rest at ease. Second, as I have already indicated, it subordinates the individual to the group in a way and to an extent that is antithetical to basic liberal values.

The relationship between liberty and equality is a complex matter into which I do not wish to enter in any detail here. Suffice it to say that there is more than one view on it. There are those like the philosopher Isaiah Berlin (1978: 81–102) who would say that while liberty and equality are both desirable ends, in an imperfect world, it is impossible to reconcile the two fully, so that some gain in the one might entail some loss in the other. On the other hand, legal theorist Ronald Dworkin (1985: 183) has said, 'I want to argue that a certain conception of equality, which I shall call the liberal conception of equality, is the nerve of liberalism.'

Some liberals will accommodate a great deal of inequality particularly where such inequality arises from competition in a formally free market. But they will not support inequalities based on race, caste, and gender, or those that are ascribed at birth, or confinement to positions of inferiority from which the individual cannot possibly escape despite his best effort. I have elsewhere (Béteille 2002: 181–203) made a distinction between 'hierarchical' and 'competitive' inequality. One can say at best that liberalism is compatible with the second but not with the first. Liberalism demands, as a very minimum, equality before the law and the equal protection of the laws.

*   *   *

From the liberal point of view, what is striking about a hierarchical society is not simply its tolerance of extreme and odious forms of inequality, but perhaps, even more, its oppressive and uncompromising subordination of the individual to the group. Inequality does not threaten liberal ideas and institutions in the same way in which the subordination of the individual to the state or the community does. It is another matter that when this subordination is carried beyond a certain point, it becomes a threat to equality and not just liberty.

Liberal ideas and values emerged in the West in the nineteenth century in response to specific economic and social conditions. They played an important part in defining the relationship between the state and the citizen. The concept of citizenship acquired increasing legal, political, and social salience in conjunction with the rise of democracy. Liberal theory sought to enlarge the rights of the citizen while at the same time setting limits to the powers of the state and its functionaries. The most important instrument created and developed for this purpose was the rule of law. The liberal ideal is to use the rule of law to ensure order and stability in society through a clear definition of the rights of the citizen.

A social order based on the rights of individuals as citizens is different from one based on castes and communities arranged according to their hierarchical status. The establishment of the rights of citizenship was accompanied by a great social churning which released the individual from the constraints of the past. It made him feel free to pursue new economic and political opportunities, although these were not in reality equally available to all. Individual mobility, both between social strata and across geographical space, greatly loosened the hold of the community over the individual.

Throughout the nineteenth century in western countries from the United States to France, there was a general sense of the advance of equality over hierarchy. This sense is best articulated in the writings of the nineteenth-century French aristocrat, Alexis de Tocqueville (1956). He noted the close relationship between individualism and equality, and expressed some anxiety that equality might grow at the expense of liberty. Tocqueville's belief that equality was growing on all fronts in the West was, of course, not wholly justified, because it can be argued that inequality in the distribution of income was on the whole increasing and not decreasing in the western countries at that time.

The illusion that equality was advancing on all fronts was sustained by the steady advance of legal equality even in the face of increasing economic inequality. A liberal social order does not require equality in every form to be established. What it does require unconditionally is equality before the law and the equal protection of the laws as well as the elimination of discrimination between individuals on arbitrary grounds such as those of race, caste, and gender.

Citizenship is incompatible with the hierarchies of estate and of caste. It is not incompatible in the same way with inequalities of class. The dialectical relationship between citizenship and social class has been examined, particularly in Britain, by a succession of sociologists from T.H. Marshall (1977) to David Lockwood (1992). In some of these writings there has been a tendency to identify citizenship with 'status' meaning 'legal' status which, of course, emphasizes equality as against 'social' status which can accommodate a great deal of inequality within the framework of legal equality (Lockwood 1996; Béteille 1996a).

In a liberal society the rule of law applies to all without consideration of birth, rank, or status. In such a society nobody is above the law, not the chief justice, not the prime minister, not even the president of the republic. It is in this context and to this extent that Dworkin's argument that liberalism must be grounded in a commitment to equality has to be understood. I would like to argue that, while liberalism is clearly opposed to hierarchy, beyond that, its attitude to equality is ambivalent. It makes many concessions to inequality of outcome despite its commitment to equality of opportunity, and sometimes on account of it.

Liberalism is uneasy about any direct or active intervention by the state for redistributing the benefits and burdens of society in the real or presumed interest of greater equality (Hayek 1963: 85–102). It is mistrustful of any action that might lead to an increase in the power of the state and the authority of its functionaries to the detriment of the rights of citizens. For it can be argued that inequality in the distribution of power is more pernicious than inequality in the distribution of income, and a policy aimed at reducing the latter might lead to an increase in the former (Béteille 2002: 164–80).

Its commitment to equality before the law and to the equal protection of the laws makes it incumbent on the liberal state to remove, by legislation where necessary, forms of disability that were commonly present in hierarchical societies, such as those against women, racial, religious, and linguistic minorities, and socially disadvantaged castes and communities. It is also obliged to remove the disabilities of bondage and servitude imposed upon individuals irrespective of race, caste, and creed; citizenship and social bondage cannot be combined in the same person. Real, as against formal, equality of opportunity requires not only the removal of disabilities but also the creation of abilities. It is here that the liberal state faces a difficult challenge in deciding how far it can interfere with the free activities of its individual citizens in order to achieve such an outcome.

A liberal society is able to accommodate a fair measure of inequality in the distribution of life chances but, in comparison with hierarchical societies, it has a bias towards equality. In a liberal society, governed by the rule of law, unequal distribution of benefits and burdens calls for some justification whereas equal distribution does not. In a hierarchical society, unequal distribution is more readily accepted as a part of the natural scheme of things. As Isaiah Berlin (1978: 99 n.1) had put it, 'Classical thought seems to be deeply and "naturally" inegalitarian.'

*   *   *

A liberal society combines the commitment to the rule of law with a commitment to the autonomy and freedom of the individual as a citizen. No society can grant its individual members absolute autonomy without any kind of restraint. Restraints on the autonomy of the individual do not all come from a single source, but from a variety of sources. In the West those restraints have been seen as coming mainly from the authority of the state and the laws made by it. However, pressures for conforming to the customs of the community and the directives of its leaders have acted and continue to act as significant restraints on the freedom of the individual in many societies, and particularly ours.

This can be easily illustrated by considering the position of women in many contemporary societies. In the past the position of a woman, as daughter, wife, and mother, was governed by the principle of perpetual tutelage: she was not free to take any individual initiative within the community or even the family. The law has now greatly enlarged the rights of women, but the customs of the community within which they live strictly forbid their taking the initiative in many matters of vital importance to them as persons. It is not so much the state as the village, the caste, and the kin group that act against such initiative.

Communities are not based only on locality. They are based also on kinship and religion. Even when the members of such a community are territorially dispersed, they are expected to carry a strong sense of their collective identity with them. In India caste is the pre-eminent example of a community of birth. Members of the same caste retain a sense of common identity despite geographical dispersion and despite social differentiation in terms of occupation, education, and income. The same is of course true of communities based on language and religion. This sense of identity serves to guide the choices that individuals make along prescribed, or at least predictable, channels.

Indian society has been likened to a mosaic of communities based on language, religion, sect, caste, and tribe. Those who value diversity for its own sake are inclined to put this on the credit side of the Indian heritage. But the other side of the picture is that membership in a community fixes the identity of the individual to a large extent, and restricts his choice of action to some extent.

What may be called 'ethnic identity' in a broad sense has some place in many, if not most, large societies. Ethnic identities have survived the melting pot in the United States and in many other countries in various stages of economic development (Glazer and Moynihan 1975). What is distinctive, not to say unique, about India is the sheer multiplicity of groups based on language, religion, caste, and tribe, and their durability in the face of major historical change.

Here I would like to distinguish between language and religion on the one hand, and caste and tribe on the other, as markers of enduring social identity. Distinctions of language are acknowledged and, indeed, valued among human beings in all societies and they have been so valued in all historical epochs. This is to some extent true also of identities based on religion which have endured despite the advance of secular ideas and institutions. When the makers of modern India were engaged in the task of building the Indian nation, they did not by any means intend to do away with differences of language or religion. Rather, they celebrated the diversity of India precisely because of its capacity to accommodate those differences.

From the liberal point of view, differences of caste and tribe do not have the same moral significance as those of language and religion. They do not contribute to the enrichment of human civilization in the same way at all. The liberal regards them as the social residues of an earlier historical epoch and hopes that they will pass away from India as similar markers of social identity have passed away elsewhere in the world.

Somewhat to the disappointment of liberal nationalists, caste has survived into the twenty-first century. It has to some extent redefined the identities of religion and language in its own image. As I have explained in an earlier essay (Béteille 2002: 59–69), the term *varna* has been displaced by the term *jati* to signify identity by birth in writings about society in many Indian languages. In languages such as Bengali and Hindi, the term jati is used to refer to groups defined by religion and language, in addition to those defined by caste (or tribe), and to communities of birth in general. Not all social identities are defined by birth; some are acquired by choice. The distinction between 'identities of birth' and 'identities of choice' is an important one to which I will return later.

*   *   *

I turn now from the multiplicity to the durability of communities of birth. I will speak here mainly of tribes and castes, and of their mutual relations. Tribes and castes are presumed to belong to different sociological types, yet in India they have been confused with each other all the time, ever since the colonial administration sought to enumerate, list, and classify the communities of India in the nineteenth century (Béteille 1998).

The continued and vigorous existence of castes has surprised some in view of the expectations created at the time of independence. What should be even more surprising is the continued presence of a very large number of tribes despite the country's recent widely acclaimed success in maintaining a healthy rate of economic growth. Students of anthropology are taught that the tribe represents not only a particular form of social organization but also a particular phase of social evolution. All societies have presumably passed through a tribal stage or a stage dominated by bands, segmentary tribes, tribal chiefdoms, and so on, which were displaced as societies advanced in scale and complexity.

We know from history that there were tribes in Germany, France, and Italy in the past. Why are there no tribes in those countries any more whereas in India, the number of tribes as well as the tribal population as a whole keeps increasing? The argument that after we achieve a high rate of economic growth and ensure that it brings about a general improvement in the material conditions of the population as a whole, the tribes and castes that are so prominent in our social landscape will simply fade away does not carry much conviction. The plain fact is that we have no satisfactory theory that can explain the relationship between economic growth and social transformation, and none that can predict the course of the latter.

Can we specify the conditions under which a tribe ceases to be a tribe, or, to put it differently, the conditions under which the population of a tribe merges with the general population and its members cease to regard themselves as belonging to one or another tribe? These conditions are difficult to specify because the process is governed by changes not only in patterns of education and employment but also in the policies adopted by the government. In recent decades, those policies have been such as to strengthen, rather than weaken, each tribe's sense of its own identity as a tribe.

Today, unlike in the past, a community is identified as a tribe by being officially listed as one in a schedule attached to the Constitution. Now, while it is possible, though becoming increasingly difficult, to add new groups to the schedule, it is impossible to remove from it any group that is already in it.

Castes have survived and will continue to survive for broadly the same reasons that have led to the survival of tribes. It is not my argument that nothing has changed in Indian society in our time. A great many things have indeed changed since the beginning of the twentieth century, and particularly since independence. We have had urbanization, industrialization, and technological advance on a considerable scale. It would hardly be noteworthy if collective identities remained intact in a society where nothing changed very much. What is noteworthy is that they have remained intact despite the many changes that Indian society is now undergoing.

Europeans who came to live and work in India as administrators, missionaries, and merchants were struck by the distinctive social landscape they encountered. Because they had come from a world whose social contours were undergoing rapid and significant change, they were struck by the fact that, while their own society was in continuous motion, Indian society remained frozen in its peculiarly rigid mould. We know with the advantage of hindsight that they exaggerated the lack of change in India. But their representation of Indian society as immutable and unchanging became the conventional wisdom among those who wrote about the country, including many Indians.

As sociologists began to look more closely at Indian society on the ground after independence and to adopt what came to be known as the 'field view' as against the 'book view' of it, they were able to see the many changes taking place in it. Moreover, they realized that such changes had been taking place in the past as well. The image of Indian society as immutable and unchanging did not fit very well with the new facts being brought to light by social anthropologists and social historians. A new generation of students of society and politics began to look for the sources of dynamism inherent in the structure of Indian society.

The turbulence in Indian society, past and present, was seen in the contest between groups over land, over power, and over status. The idea that each caste remained in its allotted place for all time was shown to be a myth. New groups were being incorporated into the larger society; old ones split and became dispersed; and there was continuous change in the social positions of groups. To be sure, these changes did not take place at the pace of the changes taking place in industrial societies. They took place in slow motion, so to say, and were therefore not immediately apparent to the casual observer.

It had been noted by N.K. Bose (1941) in a paper published before independence that the relationship between tribe and caste had been changing in India since ancient and medieval times. A group that at a certain point of time showed all the characteristics of a tribe could in course of time emerge out of its isolation, enter into closer relationship with various groups in the larger society, become a part of its social division of labour, and come to be regarded as a caste. In this process it might change its mode of livelihood, its religious practice, and its mode of speech, and still maintain, as a group, its own immutable identity. It is this that was characterized by Bose as the Hindu method of tribal absorption.

There are today some 400-odd groups designated as Scheduled Tribes in India. These groups differ among themselves in size, scale, mode of livelihood, religious practice, and social organization. Some of them number in millions and are highly differentiated in terms of occupation, education, and income. Yet they carry a strong sense of their distinctive identity which has in recent decades been reinforced by the political positions adopted by their leaders who, as one might expect, belong typically to the middle class. India now has increasing numbers of individuals who are members both of a tribe and of the middle class and who, indeed, use their tribal identity as one of the ways of advancing themselves in that class.

There was continuous rearrangement of castes, tribes, and sects within the larger social order throughout India's long history. Periods of unusual turbulence were followed by periods of relative calm, but the social order never really remained immobile and frozen within its mould. Castes and, more generally, subcastes, or even sub-subcastes or groups of lineages were continuously changing places in the social order. There were characteristic strategies for moving upwards through the process which Srinivas (1995) named as 'Sanskritization'. We may assume that there was also some downward mobility of groups, but this is difficult to establish on a firm historical basis.

While social mobility was undoubtedly present in pre-British India, what colonial rule did was to create the conditions for a new type of mobility based on success in education and employment. The basic unit of mobility in the old order was the group—the subcaste or cluster of lineages—whereas the basic unit in the new type of mobility was the individual or the household. The new type of mobility has been accompanied by the growth and expansion of a new middle class of a kind that did not exist in pre-British India.

The social churning set in motion by the expansion of the middle class and by increased opportunities for individual mobility redefines the significance of collective identities but does not necessarily extinguish them. In particular, linguistic and religious minorities continue to maintain their strength and sometimes even to augment it in the face of real or perceived threats to their survival. Today the world as a whole is witnessing a resurgence of collective identities partly in response to the fears of levelling that many feel will be the inevitable outcome of globalization. But the identities due to caste and tribe appear to derive their sustenance in India from political compulsions of a somewhat distinctive nature. At the very time when it appeared that they would wither away, they were given a new lease of life by electoral politics.

* * *

I now return to the distinction I had made earlier between identities of birth and identities of choice. It is a sociological truism that there is no country in the world in which there are only individuals at one end and the nation at the other, with nothing to stand in between. As I pointed out in an earlier essay, 'Every society has its own internal arrangements: its groups, classes and communities; its associations, organizations and institutions; and its networks of interpersonal relations, linking the different parts to each other and to the whole' (Béteille 1996b: 14). Each one of these might legitimately claim some loyalty from the individual, and not simply the community of which he is a member by birth.

There is no intrinsic reason why a lawyer cannot be as deeply attached to the court in which he practices, or the doctor to his hospital or clinic, or the scientist to his laboratory, or even the clerk to his office and the worker to his shop floor as a person may be attached to his caste, or even to the religion of his ancestors. But such attachments and loyalties vary greatly between different societies and between different historical epochs. They cannot be treated simply as matters of individual taste and preference, but depend, in addition, on the social and political conditions that shape the lives of individuals.

In a recent work on the subject, Amartya Sen (2006) has taken a strong position against what he has called the 'solitarist approach' to identity. A solitarist approach is one which singles out one specific component of an individual's identity and gives it a unique and privileged status. The component that is usually singled out is the 'religious' or 'civilizational' component which is then made to do service not just in governing the identity of the individual members of a society but for marking out the society as a whole. Sen argues, with good reason, that this peculiar representation of the world is a source of much of the violence in our time. A striking, though by no means uncommon, consequence of this is that a person often has to carry the burden of a religious identity even when he does not subscribe to the beliefs or observe the practices that define that religion. A man is thus identified as a Hindu, a Muslim, or a Christian simply because he was born as one or because his forefathers had been of that community. In the modern world those who assert their religious identity most aggressively are often the ones who are most negligent about their own religious duties.

In contrast to the solitarist approach, Sen would recommend what may be called a 'pluralist' one, which favours recognition of the many different strands in the identity of each individual and to the variety of strands that contribute differently to the identities of different individuals. Due recognition of this variety should lead each individual to choose for himself the strands out of which he will construct his own identity.

It will be readily conceded by any sociologist that the individual has multiple identities. That is the staple of what is known as role theory. Sen (2006: 19) says:

> There are a great variety of categories to which we simultaneously belong. I can be, at the same time, an Asian, an Indian citizen, a Bengali with Bangladeshi ancestry, an American or British resident, an economist, a dabbler in philosophy, an author, a Sanskritist, a strong believer in secularism and democracy, a man, a feminist, a heterosexual, a defender of gay and lesbian rights, with a non-religious lifestyle, from a Hindu background, a non-Brahmin ....

He goes on to add that he has provided only a small sample of categories to which he may simultaneously belong.

Sen makes the point that we must not regard identity as destiny but recognize that we have choices in the matter of determining our own identity for ourselves. He lists a great many categories which are not only different but diversely different. Some affiliations are passing and others are life-long. They do not all provide the individual with the same degree of freedom in either adopting or discarding them. I can choose to be or not be a feminist, and I have chosen not to be one. Having been born male, I can hardly make my choice to be a man or a woman in the same spirit. I might yearn for the life of a woman, but I will cause great dismay to my family and friends by acting as if I were one.

I would like to live in a world in which I have more freedom to choose the components of my identity than I have now. At the same time, we are all a little suspicious of individuals who feel free to adopt and discard the components of their identity according to their will and pleasure. The chameleon has its attractions, but it is not everybody's favourite animal.

Within the same society individuals differ very much in their willingness to discard old components of their identity and adopt new ones. Nor is it a matter of willingness alone, for one must also have the ability to move from one position to another. There is always some risk in turning one's back on an old identity and reaching out for a new one which appears more rewarding or more exciting. Not everyone can move backwards and forwards with equal ease in a society in which life chances are distributed very unequally among individuals.

The choices open to an individual in constructing his own identity vary considerably according to his social location. Even his awareness of the choices available varies. No doubt every individual has some choice in the matter, but we cannot make our choices in a rational manner if we believe that our freedom is unlimited and our choices unconstrained. Individuals differ not only in their personal endowments but also in the material, cultural, and social capital at their disposal, and these differences influence the extent to which they are able to construct their own identities.

Every individual is born into a pre-existing social arrangement. As he passes from infancy to old age, he acquires not only new capacities but also new obligations. His very conception of his own self is to some extent shaped by the social environment within which he must act. 'No man is an Island, entire of itself' is not just a poetic conceit; it is a profound sociological truth. It is not at all my argument that attachments acquired at birth are or should be more binding than those acquired through the exercise of conscious choice, in the office, in the factory, or in the neighbourhood, but even the latter cannot be discarded or abandoned without any personal or social cost. I can think of any number of individuals—honest Indians all of them—who feel more strongly attached to their college, their office, or their regiment than to their caste or their ancestral religion.

Apart from individual variations, there are significant differences among societies in their dominant traditions and values. Some social traditions have a much stronger bias for identities of birth, and exercise greater vigilance in safeguarding the obligations that arise from them. To be sure, in any large and complex society there is always room for individuals to follow their own inclinations and form attachments of choice to which they transfer some of their loyalties. But individualism itself is a social value that is not viewed with the same favour in all societies (Tocqueville 1956; Dumont 1977).

In India, the individual's wish to live his own life according to his own sense of what he is best fitted to do is often viewed as nothing short of selfishness.

The bias in favour of collective identities in general and identities of birth in particular need not remain fixed for ever in a social tradition. Alexis de Tocqueville (1956) wrote memorably about the way in which the social bias shifted from the group to the individual as western societies moved from aristocracy to democracy. Economic and social arrangements changed; the laws changed; and, above all, there was a change in the climate of opinion and in what Tocqueville memorably called 'the habits of the heart'.

Can the habits of the heart be changed by a sustained rate of economic growth or by intelligent social policy? Colonial rule introduced a new legal order and new economic opportunities in the nineteenth century. Those two in conjunction initiated a process of social churning which led to the emergence of a new educational and occupational system, and a new middle class. The social churning opened to view a new horizon of possibilities for those who entered the middle class or aspired to enter it. But the scope of those changes remained highly restricted, and barely altered the social categories, not to speak of the habits of the heart, of the large masses of people who continued without the benefits that the new types of education and employment offered.

The new middle class, no matter how tiny its size in relation to the general population, was not averse to exploring the possibilities of individual mobility. But this does not mean that its members were prepared to give up the safety, the security, and the comforts which they could draw from the community to which they belonged by birth. The extended family, the lineage, and even the subcaste remained very much a part of their social imagination even when they contemplated the prospects of success through education and employment in the services, in the professions, and in business. The successful individual was expected to carry some of his past obligations with him, and he often did so. Those who neglected or repudiated such obligations were regarded as morally inadequate, no matter how large their worldly success.

The trends of change during the decades leading up to the independence of India did not all move in the same direction. There was some movement of individuals across the social space, leading to a loosening of the hold of the community over its individual members. But there were contrary trends as well, bringing rival communities in contention with each other and thereby enhancing, and not reducing, the individual's consciousness of the community of which he was a member by birth. The conflicts between religious communities and between groups of castes made it difficult for individuals to lose sight of the groups which claimed their allegiance. Where an individual is a member of a backward caste or a religious minority, his reluctance to stand up for the community to which he belongs is treated as a sign of moral weakness.

* * *

At the time of independence, India stood at a crossroads. As I have pointed out repeatedly, it had been for centuries a society of castes and communities while the leaders of independent India wished to make it into a nation of citizens. In that they put their trust on the compulsions of economic development and the liberating promise of democracy.

They were of course aware that caste and community had been used in the political process during colonial rule and that politics had been used to reinforce and not weaken the consciousness of the divisions among them. But they were optimistic about what democratic politics could contribute in independent India to the building of new associations and institutions whose operation would be governed by the free choices made by individuals rather than the compulsions of caste and community. And, of course, they believed that in this, democratic politics and economic development would work hand in hand and never at cross purposes.

As it turned out, democratic politics did not lead to the effacement of caste consciousness, but gave it a new lease of life. At first the pace of economic growth was slow and halting, but a steady and perhaps sustainable increase in it now seems evident. But, as in the case of democratic politics, economic development cannot be guaranteed to remove caste from the minds of people. Economic development is not about growth alone, but also about the distribution of the fruits of growth. Now there is a world of difference between policies that take individuals and households as units and those that take castes and communities as units in seeking a fair and just distribution of the fruits of economic growth. It would be unreasonable to expect politicians who have used caste so actively in mobilizing electoral support to ignore it in considering equitable distribution. It is thus that the simple word 'justice' has come to be replaced by the more sonorous phrase 'social justice' meaning parity between castes and communities.

Indian society has been an unequal society since time immemorial. Colonial rule did not lead to any significant reduction of inequality, but the argument that it led to an increase in it has to be treated with some scepticism. Democracy brought in political equality of a sort, but that only made the social and economic inequalities that remained appear even more glaring. During the struggle for independence the leaders of the nationalist movement put the responsibility for the extremes of inequality on colonial rule. When independence came, the removal of inequality or at least a substantial reduction in it became their major concern.

The inequalities by which Indian society was marked were of many different kinds. There were inequalities of income and wealth between individuals and households which may be broadly described as inequalities of class. As I have already pointed out, citizenship and social class stand in a contrapuntal relationship in all democratic societies. But, in addition to the inequalities of class based on income and wealth, there were also the disparities between groups marked by social exclusion of which the practice of untouchability was the most extreme form. The central place occupied by the ritual opposition of purity and pollution in the Hindu religious tradition gave a peculiarly rigid and elaborate form to the distinctions of social status.

Nehru believed and the majority of planners and policymakers associated with the new government also believed that the roots of the inequality in the distribution of life chances in India, as elsewhere in the poorer countries, lay in the economic order. One reason for focusing on inequalities of income and wealth was that it appeared relatively easy to formulate policies for their redress. It was hoped that, with a turnaround in the economic order, social disparities based on age-old prejudices would be effectively reduced. It is in this light that we can see why measures for economic reform were given more weight than measures for social reform in the early years of planning and policy-making.

In this concluding section I will consider briefly two major policy initiatives undertaken by the government immediately after independence with the objective of reducing inequalities and disparities in the interest of equity and social justice. The first is agrarian reform which addresses issues of class without seeking to directly affect the disparities between castes. The second is positive discrimination which seeks to reduce the disparities between castes without directly addressing questions of class. Both initiatives had their origins in the period of colonial rule, but their scope was expanded greatly after independence.

The agrarian social structure in India was marked by huge inequalities between households in the ownership, control, and use of land. At the top were a few landowning families, usually, but not necessarily, belonging to the highest castes, which owned or controlled vast amounts of land which they themselves did not till. At the bottom were the masses of landless agricultural labourers who neither owned nor controlled the land on which they worked and that was necessary for their survival. In between were various categories of non-cultivating lessees, owner-cultivators, cultivating tenants, and sharecroppers of various kinds (Béteille 1975).

There were two principal objectives of land reforms: the abolition of intermediaries and the transfer of land to the tiller. They were designed to benefit households with little or no land at the expense of those with abundant land, particularly where that land was not cultivated with household labour but through tenancy and wage labour. Similar programmes of agrarian reform were being adopted, with similar objectives, in many different countries at about the same time (Warriner 1969).

Agrarian reform had a wide measure of support in the early years
of independence among planners, policymakers, social scientists, and
the intelligentsia in general (Thorner 1956). It was viewed by them
as a progressive measure that would contribute not only to equity
but also to efficiency in production. There was not the same kind
of enthusiasm at that time for quotas in education and employment
based on caste and community. Apart from the commitment to
the Scheduled Castes and the Scheduled Tribes written into the
Constitution, the demands made by or on behalf of other castes and
communities were viewed by many as being backward-looking, and,
in effect if not in intention, socially divisive.

The attitude of the Congress leadership towards quotas based on
caste and community had been negative, if not hostile, during the
nationalist movement. After the bitter experience of the Partition, it
was hesitant to do anything that might revive the consciousness of
caste and community in public life. At the same time, the disparities
between castes remained, and could not be wished out of existence.
The government set up a Backward Classes Commission under Kaka
Kalelkar in 1954, but the Commission was divided in its views, and
its recommendations remained infructuous.

The misgiving about reviving caste consciousness even in a good
cause is evident in the attitude of Kaka Kalelkar, the chairman of
the first Backward Classes Commission. He went along with the
recommendation of the majority in support of caste quotas, but his
heart was not in it. In a letter forwarding the report of the Commission
to the President of India, he pointed to the pre-eminent value to be
placed on the nation at one end and the citizen at the other, and
wrote that 'nothing should be allowed to organize itself between
these two ends to the detriment of the freedom of the individual and
the solidarity of the nation' (GoI 1956: iv).

The political climate began to change in the 1960s and the
1970s, and became more accommodating of the divisions of caste
and community and the articulation of those divisions in public life.
The use of caste for the mobilization of electoral support became
more open and more widespread. It took a little time for our public
intellectuals to recognize what was happening on the ground.

Here our politicians were in advance of our intellectuals, and they took the lead in taking caste into account in making their political calculations and bargains. In the last couple of decades the electronic media have taken up the theme of caste, and played an important part in bringing the divisions of caste into the public consciousness. For every hour devoted to discussing the disparities between castes and communities, not even five minutes are spent on the description and analysis of the inequalities of income and wealth between individuals.

At first the use of caste was accepted on pragmatic grounds. Where some parties were using it for gathering electoral support, the others could not stand by and watch their own support being depleted by their rivals. It soon turned out that the identities of caste, being clear and easily recognizable, could be more effectively used in electoral politics than those of class whose boundaries were far from clear in an agrarian society. Even the left parties realized that the language of caste resonated more strongly in their electorate than that of class.

Soon the language of social justice was introduced to reinforce the claims made on behalf of various castes and communities—the backward castes and then the religious minorities—in the public domain. The second Backward Classes Commission in 1980 under Mr B.P. Mandal became a turning point in the public debate about caste and social justice (GoI 1980). Mr Mandal had set about his task in a very different spirit from that of Kaka Kalelkar. Mr Mandal's commission made strong recommendations for quotas in education and employment on the basis of caste. He made it clear in his report that social justice in India required that each community be given its due share of the benefits irrespective of the gains and losses of the individual members of society. Those who questioned the merits of caste quotas were put on the back foot by being represented as opponents of social justice. All political parties, not least the parties of the left, have given their endorsement to the case made by Mr Mandal. The politics of caste has clearly displaced the politics of class, at least for the present.

It is difficult to say how far the disparities between castes and communities have in fact been reduced by the policy of reservation.

But what is undeniable is that stark and glaring inequalities of income and wealth continue to exist between individuals and households. Such inequalities act against the creation of citizenship except in a purely nominal sense. It is not a liberal society which neglects economic inequalities between citizens in order to promote social and political parity between castes.

References

Berlin, Isaiah. 1978. *Concepts and Categories*. London: The Hogarth Press.

Béteille, André. 1975. *Studies in Agrarian Social Structure*. New Delhi: Oxford University Press.

―――. 1996a. 'The Mismatch between Class and Status', *The British Journal of Sociology*, vol. 47, no. 3, pp. 513–26.

―――. 1996b. *Civil Society and Its Institutions*. Calcutta: USEFI.

―――. 1998. 'The Idea of Indigenous People', *Current Anthropology*, vol. 39, no. 2, pp. 187–91.

―――. 2002. *Equality and Universality*. New Delhi: Oxford University Press.

Bose, N.K. 1941. 'The Hindu Method of Tribal Absorption', *Science and Culture*, vol. 7, no. 4, pp. 188–94.

Dumont, Lewis. 1977. *From Mandeville to Marx*. Chicago: University of Chicago Press.

Dworkin, Ronald. 1985. *A Matter of Principle*. Cambridge, Mass.: Harvard University Press.

Glazer N. and D.P. Moynihan (ed.). 1975. *Ethnicity*. Cambridge, Mass.: Harvard University Press.

Government of India (GoI). 1956. *Report of the Backward Classes Commission 1955*. New Delhi (Chairman: Kaka Kalelkar).

―――. 1980. *Report of the Backward Classes Commission*. New Delhi (Chairman: B.P. Mandal).

Hayek, F.A. 1963. *The Constitution of Liberty*. London: Routledge and Kegan Paul.

Lockwood, David. 1992. *Solidarity and Schism*. Oxford: Clarendon Press.

―――. 1996. 'Civic Integration and Class Formation', *The British Journal of Sociology*, vol. 47, no. 3, pp. 531–50.

Marshall, T.H. 1977. *Class, Citizenship and Social Development.* Chicago: University of Chicago Press.

Sen, Amartya. 2006. *Identity and Violence.* New York: Norton.

Srinivas, M.N. 1995. *Social Change in Modern India.* New Delhi: Orient Longman.

Thorner, Daniel. 1956. *The Agrarian Prospect in India.* Delhi: Delhi School of Economics.

Tocqueville, Alexis de. 1956. *Democracy in America.* New York: Alfred Knopf, 2 vols.

Warriner, Doreen. 1969. *Land Reform in Principle and Practice.* London: Oxford University Press.

8

Law and Custom

The distinction between law and custom is as important as it is difficult to make and maintain in a consistent way. There is perhaps in every society some disjunction between the two, but the disjunction becomes most conspicuous in societies that are in transition or are undergoing rapid social change. This is the case with us in India today where we have created laws based on the principle of equality whereas our customs are permeated by hierarchical ideas, beliefs, and values.

Our predicament is not unique although it is in many ways distinctive. In a remarkable study of democracy in America made nearly 200 years ago, Alexis de Tocqueville drew attention to the difference between law and custom. His focus was on the United States, but Europe, particularly his own country France, was never far from his thoughts. He asked what contributed to the success of democracy in America as compared with its uneven progress in Europe. He pointed to three sets of factors: (i) the accidents of geography and history; (ii) the creation of good laws; and (iii) the presence of congenial customs. He wrote: 'These three great causes serve, no doubt, to regulate and direct American democracy; but if they were to be classed in their proper order, I should say that physical circumstances are less efficient than the laws, and the laws infinitely less so than the customs of the people' (Tocqueville 1945: I, 322).

What will be the predicament of a society where the laws support democracy but the customs do not?

Tocqueville went on to add:

> I am convinced that the most advantageous situation and the best possible laws cannot maintain a constitution in spite of the customs of a country; while the latter may turn to some advantage the most unfavourable positions and the worst laws. The importance of customs is a common truth to which study and experience incessantly direct our attention. (Ibid.)

This way of looking at the matter is likely to appeal much more to social anthropologists than to jurists and lawyers, whether they are proponents of legal positivism or of theories of natural law. Social anthropologists have been at pains to show for over a hundred years that customs are not created by the command of any sovereign and also that there is nothing natural about the varieties of customs by which human beings have felt themselves bound at various places and in various times.

In pointing to the primacy of custom over law, Tocqueville gave the term an inclusive meaning. He said:

> I use the word *customs* with the meaning the ancients attached to the word *mores*; for I apply it not only to manners properly so called—that is to what might be termed the habits of the heart—but to the various notions and opinions current among men and to the mass of those ideas which constitute their character of mind (Ibid.: I, 299).

As I have noted, the disjunction between law and custom becomes marked under conditions of change. It is not at all my argument that only laws change whereas customs never do. My argument is two-fold. First, the rhythms of change for custom are not the same as they are for law, particularly in the contemporary world. Second, our understanding of the causes and conditions of change is far less clear in the case of custom than in that of law. This is in part because conscious, deliberate, and purposeful action contributes far more to changes in law than to changes in custom. As a matter of fact, even though social anthropologists have devoted themselves to the systematic study of custom for well over a hundred years, they know very little as to why customs change and how new customs may be created to replace old ones.

New laws may be enacted for a variety of reasons. The modern state, constituted on the principle of the rule of law, places a high value on uniformity and consistency. Sometimes the existing laws are in conflict with each other. The state then feels the need to create new laws where those are required to eliminate or reduce inconsistencies among existing ones. Lord Macaulay, as the law member on the viceroy's council had said, 'Our principle is simply this; uniformity where you can have it; diversity where you must have it; but in all cases certainty' (Stokes 1959: 219–20).

New laws may be needed to meet new economic requirements. British rule introduced many economic innovations in India. This required the enactment of new laws, particularly in regard to property (Guha 1963). Land revenue administration became an important part of colonial rule as it had been of Mughal rule in earlier times. The new laws introduced by the British altered the relations arising from the ownership, control, and use of land. As inevitably happens in such cases, the consequences of the new laws were different from the intentions with which they were enacted. One of the unanticipated consequences of new legislation is to bring about long-term changes in the customs of people.

The colonial administration was more hesitant to interfere with social customs, such as those relating to caste and gender, and the hesitation increased after 1857. In any event, the British did not have any general plan to bring about a radical change in the structure of Indian society. They recognized the fact that Indian society was a society of castes and communities and one marked by the perpetual tutelage of women, and they were quite willing to let the social order remain where it was. Their objective was to maintain law and order and stability, and not to take too many chances with plans for social transformation.

The restraints which the colonial administration had imposed on itself in its own interest were removed with the attainment of independence. The mood then was the one expressed eloquently by Nehru in his memorable 'Tryst with Destiny' speech in which he exhorted the nation to seize the moment 'which comes but rarely … when we step out from the old to the new, when an age ends, and when the soul of a nation long suppressed finds utterance' (Nehru 1949: 25).

The process whereby the soul of the nation was to find utterance had already begun in the Constituent Assembly. As I have pointed out earlier (Chapter 6 in this volume), the objective was to transform a society of castes and communities into a nation of citizens, an objective that no colonial government would set for itself. The new government set about creating a whole range of new laws that were designed to undermine the hierarchies of caste and gender. These laws have often had to encounter strong resistance from customs rooted in immemorial tradition. Where the laws cannot be enforced and are wilfully ignored or bypassed, the credibility of the legislative process itself comes into question. While legislation can play a useful part in directing social change, its indiscriminate use for that purpose can be counterproductive.

* * *

The study of law and custom has been by convention divided between scholars with very different intellectual orientations. Law has generally been studied in societies with well-defined institutions such as the state and the church. The systematic study of custom, on the other hand, began with the study of small, simple, preliterate societies that were either stateless or had states of the most rudimentary kind. These societies were commonly described, even by some anthropologists who studied them, as existing in a condition of 'ordered anarchy' so that there one had little choice but to study custom.

Whether or not law in the strict sense of the term exists in all societies depends to some extent on the meaning we give to the term. This is a question to which I will return soon. For the present it is important to note that there is a difference between societies that do and those that do not have legal specialists. Among legal specialists I include not only judges with prescribed duties and benefits of office, but also lawyers and jurists. The presence of legal specialists contributes to the systematization and codification of law and, through that process, to its differentiation from custom.

It is not that legal scholars have never turned their attention to custom. The names of such great scholars as Maine (1931), Maitland (Pollock and Maitland 1968), and Vinogradoff (1905) come readily to mind. But their main interest in custom was historical rather than analytical. They wanted to show how law gradually evolved out of custom. My principal interest, on the other hand, is to examine how the two co-exist with their divergent aims and tendencies within the same society.

One important consequence of the growth of legal specialists from medieval or even ancient times to our own is that there are today many different concepts of law. It is well known, if not notorious, that Professor Ronald Dworkin who succeeded Professor H.L.A. Hart as professor of jurisprudence at Oxford had a conception of law that differed considerably from that of his predecessor for whom he, nevertheless, expressed the highest regard (Dworkin 1984: 7–13). Professor Hart (1970: 1–12) had himself pointed out that few intellectual disciplines have been bedevilled by the problem of definition as much as the discipline of law.

In what follows, I will stay with the approach to law associated with legal positivism. Legal positivism has been criticized for its narrowness, and its attempt to maintain a strict separation between law and morality has been condemned as sterile. Nevertheless, it has pursued a certain line of thinking from John Austin to H.L.A. Hart which is relatively easy for the non-specialist to follow. Moreover, I believe that legal positivism provides the best starting point for someone who wishes to understand and explain the difference between law and custom.

I would like to discuss in some detail the concept of law as elaborated by Professor Hart. I need not repeat the point already made that it is only one among several conceptions of law, but will only say that it is neither eccentric nor idiosyncratic. It has the advantage of being clearly articulated in a manner that makes it easy to determine what law is and what it is not. In this conception, law is distinguished clearly from morality and from custom. I will have more to say as I go along about the distinction made explicitly between law and custom, a distinction that is implicit in the writings of most authorities on the subject of law.

Hart begins with Austin's famous maxim that 'law is the command of the sovereign', but finds that proposition in its bare form to be inadequate. His focus shifts, through a series of carefully constructed moves, from commands to rules. Having established that in dealing with law we have to deal with a set of rules rather than instincts, intuitions, perceptions, sentiments, or ideals, he addresses the fact that those rules are not all of the same kind. It is the recognition of the heterogeneous nature of the rules of law that marks the departure in Hart's approach from that of Austin. It also enables Hart to elucidate the transition from a 'pre-legal' world governed by custom and morality to a 'legal' one in which law displaces custom (though not morality) to a large extent. Here Hart belongs clearly within that tradition of historical jurisprudence in which custom and law represent successive evolutionary phases.

Law, according to Hart (Ibid.: 77–96), is a union of primary and secondary rules. These two sets of rules are not of the same kind although there is a close relationship between them. The primary rules, though necessary and indispensable, cannot by themselves constitute a mature system of law. Law in the proper sense of the term emerges only when a set of secondary rules becomes added to the primary ones. In a small, homogeneous community where the same rules of social interchange are acknowledged and observed by all or most of its individual members, no separate agency or mechanism is required to ensure compliance with them.

But as society expands and becomes more complex, 'the primary rules of obligation' can no longer work to the satisfaction of all. A new set of rules, of a distinct nature, which Hart describes as 'secondary rules', becomes necessary. 'They specify the ways in which the primary rules may be conclusively ascertained, introduced, eliminated, varied, and the fact of their violation conclusively determined' (Ibid.: 92). It must be clearly understood that the secondary rules do not supplant the primary ones but only supplement them.

A regime which is governed solely by the primary rules of mutual obligation suffers from several deficiencies which can be addressed only by the creation of secondary rules. First, there is uncertainty in the regime of primary rules for which it is necessary to create 'rules of recognition' to enable people to know what the relevant rule is. Second, the static nature of the regime of primary rules has to be addressed by creating 'rules of change'. Third, the inefficiency of the diffuse pressure through which grievances are redressed has to be addressed by creating 'rules of adjudication'. It is in this way that we move from the pre-legal to the legal world, or from customs to statutes.

In a pre-legal system, the task of identifying what the custom is can be met by most adult members of the community, or at least most adult male members of it. No specialized agency is required for the purpose. 'In a modern legal system where there are a variety of "sources" of law, the rule of recognition is correspondingly more complex: the criteria for identifying the law are multiple and commonly include a written constitution, enactment by a legislature, and judicial precedents' (Ibid.: 98). Law is no longer embedded in society in the way that custom is. It becomes differentiated to a greater or lesser extent from the other aspects of society and acquires a life of its own under the care of legal specialists.

Hart goes on to say, 'In our own system, custom and precedent are subordinate to legislation since customary and common law may be deprived of their status as law by statute' (Ibid.). Here we see an attitude that is characteristic not only of legal positivists but of legal scholars in general. Law is in its nature dynamic and progressive whereas custom carries the burden of inertia. Custom may be valuable in its own way, but wherever there is a conflict between custom and law, it is law that must prevail.

The union of primary and secondary rules is facilitated greatly by the use of the written word. The command of the sovereign is one thing when it is tacitly acknowledged and accepted by all or most persons to whom it is meant to apply. It is a very different thing when it is written down in the form of a statute. Societies vary greatly in the extent to which they use the written word for recording the rules by which their members are required to be bound. In addition, the written word itself is not assigned the same value in all societies, including societies whose members may be familiar with its use.

In India today legal rules derive their ultimate authority from a written constitution. A written constitution is of course not indispensable to the operation of a fully formed legal system. The United Kingdom provides a well-known example of a legal system which has worked well for centuries without a written constitution. India provides an example of the opposite kind. Our legal system does not work very smoothly despite the presence of a written constitution produced with the most elaborate care.

The Constitution of India was written at a turning point in the life of the nation as it prepared to move from colonial rule to self-rule. It was designed to be a marker and a symbol of that turning point. The draft constitution which was discussed extensively in the Constituent Assembly was criticized from many sides. It was criticized by some for borrowing wholesale from the Government of India Act of 1935 which, after all, was the creation of colonial rule, and by others for not paying enough heed to India's ancient and glorious tradition. In the end, it turned out to be a lengthy and unwieldy charter which has had to be amended over and over again.

In the modern world, law and legislation are closely united with each other. The creation of secondary rules goes hand in hand with the creation of specialized institutions such as legislatures, courts, and administrative organs of various kinds. Such institutions had of course existed in pre-British times during which they had evolved slowly and gradually, and generally in agreement with custom rather than against it. Colonial rule introduced new legal principles and, along with them, new legal institutions which have not always fitted well into the existing social environment. The rules of their operation have often been contrary to age-old social practices based on the sentiments of kinship, caste, and community.

The institutions for the administration of the law created under colonial rule and greatly expanded since independence do not work in the manner intended or expected, particularly at the lower levels, in the districts and further down. They are subjected to contradictory pulls and pressures. The new laws are secular and impersonal and are intended to operate without considerations of kinship, caste, and community. But such considerations are deeply ingrained in the hearts and minds of those through whose agency the law has to be administered.

There is today a wide gulf between law and custom in regard to gender and caste. In the past both law and custom accommodated discrimination on the basis of caste as well as gender to a large extent. Such discrimination was considered as a part of the natural scheme of things. There was in pre-British India a great diversity of legal principle and practice. Hindu law in particular took a tolerant view of such diversity, and, where there was divergence between the classical (or *shastric*) law and custom, it often allowed the latter to prevail. As the statement by Macaulay quoted earlier indicated, this diversity could not easily be legislated out of existence.

The attitude of modern Indian law to discrimination on social grounds, whether of gender or of caste, is very different from the attitudes accommodated by law and custom in the past. It debars discrimination on those grounds except where it can be justified on grounds of equality or fairness. But, although the law has changed, the old habits of the heart continue to maintain their hold over those who have to administer it. This is an important reason why the legal machinery in India remains clogged and cases—and not just those where caste and gender are involved—remain unattended for years.

* * *

Whereas the study of law has been the province of jurists and lawyers, the systematic study of custom has been the work mainly of social anthropologists. Social anthropology began with the study of small, preliterate bands and tribes in Australia, Melanesia, Africa, and the reservations of North America. Although the range of societies studied by social anthropologists has expanded greatly since World War II, the orientation acquired by the discipline in its formative years continues to influence its current practice. When, after decolonization, anthropologists moved in large numbers from the study of tribes to the study of peasants, they retained their focus on custom to a large extent.

In the early phase of its study of preliterate bands and tribes, anthropology paid little attention to law, or, indeed to any kind of socially acknowledged rules for the regulation of life. They were divided between those who believed that primitive man lived in a state of pure anarchy and those who maintained that he simply followed custom blindly and without any thought. Intensive fieldwork through the method of participant-observation changed this. Anthropologists learnt a great deal about law and custom in tribal societies that they carried over into their study of the peasantry and that deepened the understanding of all societies including the most advanced ones.

Even after intensive fieldwork had become an established practice, not all social anthropologists believed that wherever there were rules for the regulation of social life, we could speak of law. Evans-Pritchard, who pioneered the study of segmentary political systems in Africa, raised a sceptical voice. He said, 'In a strict sense Nuer have no law. There are conventional compensations for damage, adultery, loss of limb, and so forth, but there is no authority with power to adjudicate in such matters or to enforce a verdict' (Evans-Pritchard 1940: 163). His argument was that there can be no law where there are no institutions for rule adjudication and rule enforcement. There were, nevertheless, socially recognized procedures for the settlement of disputes and the maintenance of order. In Evans-Pritchard's words, the Nuer lived in a state of 'ordered anarchy'.

The case for acknowledging the presence of law in primitive societies was made most forcefully by Malinowski (1926) who was Evans-Pritchard's teacher and had pioneered the study of such societies through the method of participant-observation. Max Gluckman, Evans-Pritchard's junior contemporary, who pioneered the study of legal anthropology in Britain, recommended a flexible approach and drew attention to the thin line separating law and custom.

The tradition of defining 'law' as what courts will enforce has thus logically produced an attempt to isolate enforcing mechanisms in societies that lack courts, and to define as 'law' any rule or obligation to which these apply. This tendency accompanies an attempt to differentiate law from custom, as if they have to be quite separate categories. (Gluckman 1965: 198)

The study of law and custom in Africa and elsewhere among tribal communities was undertaken by anthropologists in the shadow of colonial rule when new legal institutions and practices were being superimposed on existing ones that were very different in their character and origin. It was natural for colonial administrators to regard their own rules and practices as law, and to relegate to the domain of custom the rules and practices of those under their care. It goes to the credit of the anthropologists, including several who started as administrators, that they revealed the ambiguity of the distinction between the two.

It was Malinowski who took the lead in bringing the existence of primitive law to wide scholarly attention. He made his case in his characteristically assertive manner. He said that when he spoke of 'law', he did not use the term in some vague metaphorical sense but in a strictly scientific sense.

> We shall see that by an inductive examination of facts, carried out without any preconceived idea or ready-made definition, we shall be enabled to arrive at a scientific classification of the norms and rules of a primitive community, at a clear distinction of primitive law from other forms of custom, and at a new dynamic conception of the social organization of savages. (Malinowski 1926: 15–6)

Malinowski was always ready to confound his critics by throwing at them the facts about a community in whose life he had participated over an extended period of time.

For Malinowski, the supreme test of the presence of law lay in its breach and the consequences that generally, though not inevitably, followed the breach. Primitive man, like human beings everywhere, was jealous of his rights, felt bound by his obligations, and was calculating about both. There is always some uncertainty about rights and obligations because they are not likely to be perceived in the same way by all the parties concerned. No system of laws, no matter how carefully constructed, can do away with such uncertainty once and for all. It is to this uncertainty that Malinowski drew attention repeatedly in his account of law in the Trobriand Islands.

It is true that the rules of law become more elaborate and in some sense more precise with the development of what Hart calls secondary as against primary rules. As I have already indicated, writing makes a difference in this respect. But the multiplicity and elaborateness of the rules, and their formulation as statutes, do not necessarily lead to greater certainty in their application. In a large, complex, and changing society, the citizen cannot easily count on the law, no matter how precise or how accurate it may be, for delivering justice to him. This is particularly true where law and custom are at variance with each other or where the rules derive their authority from more than one source.

For the social anthropologist studying the simpler societies, whether of tribals or of peasants, the most significant aspect of the law is its socially binding nature rather than the clarity, the detail, or the precision with which its rules are formulated. Malinowski made a distinction between 'criminal' and 'civil' law in tribal societies. He sought to stress that such societies had civil and not just criminal law. He said:

> 'Civil law', the positive law governing all phases of tribal life, consists then of a body of binding obligations, regarded as a right by one party and acknowledged as a duty by the other, kept in force by a specific mechanism of reciprocity and publicity inherent in the structure of their society. These rules of civil law are elastic and possess a certain latitude. They offer not only penalties for failure, but also premiums for an overdose of fulfilment. (Ibid.: 58)

Malinowski was inclined to adopt extreme positions. The same or similar views were expressed in more moderate fashion by Radcliffe-Brown (1952: 212–9) in a brief article first published just a few years after Malinowski's work. Radcliffe-Brown adopted a clear and consistent view of social structure which he defined as a set of roles and relations based on acknowledged rights and obligations. His strong interest in the relationship between law and social structure and in the comparative method led him to take a sceptical attitude towards the view that all systems of law were basically the same. He believed that the distinction between criminal and civil law did not apply well to primitive societies and recommended in its place the distinction between the laws of public and private delicts.

Radcliffe-Brown's discussion of primitive law has to be seen in the wider context of his understanding of social sanctions. He adopted a classification of sanctions that was greatly influenced by the work of Durkheim, but Radcliffe-Brown had the advantage of first-hand acquaintance with primitive societies which Durkheim lacked. He classified sanctions along two axes, as diffuse and organized sanctions, and again as negative and positive sanctions. It is only when sanctions are organized in a certain way that they have the force of law whether or not they are in the form of written codes.

*   *   *

In the light of all that has been said earlier, the question will naturally arise as to what really is the significance of the distinction between custom and law. Why would one wish to make such a distinction at all?

One can visualize two kinds of relationship between custom and law. The first is their relationship in a relatively homogeneous social and cultural environment in which changes take place in both, but along a relatively smooth and even course. Here custom gradually evolves into law through systematization, rationalization, and codification, and the development of what Hart has described as secondary rules. In such a situation there are still many rules that remain outside the ambit of codified law. There may even be some friction between what is governed by custom and what is required by law, but the two are not necessarily regulated by contradictory principles.

This was basically the situation that Tocqueville encountered in early nineteenth-century America. That country as he saw it in 1831–2 was not internally riven by the kind of conflicts over norms and values that divided republicans from monarchists in France. France had had a revolution from which Tocqueville's own family had suffered. The leaders of its revolution wished to create radically new laws which would put an end to the old feudal customs by which France had been governed for centuries. They sought not only to recast all social relations in a new mould, but they even created a new calendar to replace the old one.

Even in Europe the relationship between custom and law did not follow the same trajectory in every country. England did not have the kind of revolution that France experienced. At the same time, there have been innumerable changes in both custom and law in England from the time of the Magna Carta to the present. England changed from a monarchy to a commonwealth and then back again to a monarchy in the seventeenth century. There were changes in land tenure and property rights; in marriage rules and in the position of women; and in the obligations owed by subordinates to their superiors. Sometimes the law changed first and then practice fell in line. But it also happened that the slow operation of economic and social forces led to changes in customary practices and the law had then to adjust itself to those changes.

The situation is different when a legal system nurtured in a particular social and cultural environment is introduced from the outside into an alien environment with its own laws and customs. A conflict of norms and values which is often deeper than what one sees in a revolution from within is generally, if not invariably, the outcome. Two hundred years of colonial rule in the countries of Asia and Africa provide many examples of this.

It was natural for the colonial administrators to believe at first that the rules that prevailed in their own country were rules of law whereas the natives whom they had brought under their care lived either in a state of anarchy or in obedience to custom. There were vast differences among the countries that made up their far-flung empire. Many lacked any kind of literary tradition, and here the presumption would be that they might have custom but were not bound within a framework of law. But it did not take them long to discover that in a country like India elaborate systems of codified law had existed for centuries. But even in India the law as it was actually administered followed more often an oral than a written tradition.

The British in India soon came to see that law and custom were intertwined in the most complex and confusing manner. They sought the assistance of native experts not only in interpreting the law but also in codifying and systematizing it. This had to be done in the interest of efficient administration, but some also took a genuine intellectual interest in native law and custom. For this they learnt not only the vernacular languages in current use but also classical languages such as Sanskrit and Persian. There were among them not only outstanding ethnographers but also outstanding classical scholars.

The colonial rulers of India sought not only to understand, interpret, and apply the existing law but also to reform the system in the light of their own laws which they considered, naturally enough, to be the most enlightened in the world. It is not as if the men who ruled India were all agreed on reforming the laws of the land. Many different positions were taken on this. There were those who believed that the laws should be left just as they were and there were others who wanted wholesale change. The Utilitarians Jeremy Bentham and James Mill were major sources of inspiration (Stokes 1959). Given the circumstances of the encounter between India and Britain in the nineteenth century, we can say with the advantage of hindsight that the advance of English law over the laws of the land was inevitable. The sheer intellectual power of that law made the advance irresistible.

India has a long and impressive intellectual tradition, but that tradition was below its peak when the encounter with the West took place. Even at its peak, the science of jurisprudence did not have a prominent place in it. Indians were unrivalled in disciplines such as mathematics, grammar, logic, and metaphysics, but they did not go very far with the study of law and its application in everyday life.

The British brought with them a new idea of the rule of law which had no real counterpart in any of the legal systems prevalent in the country. This must be counted as a permanent legacy of British rule in India. It is on this idea of the rule of law, and not the idea of *varnashramadharma* which was the basis of the classical law of India, that the Constitution of India came to be written. Although it has acquired considerable appeal among lawyers, judges, and jurists in contemporary India, it has not laid to rest the ideas, beliefs, values, and sentiments that provided the foundations of both custom and law in the past. It is this that lies at the heart of what I have elsewhere described as the conflict of norms and values in contemporary India (Béteille 1998).

The attractions of a legal order based on the rule of law soon became apparent to the new intelligentsia that emerged in the country in the wake of British rule. Some of the most gifted among them went to the law colleges in Calcutta, Bombay, and Madras, and from there on to London to qualify for the bar. The law that they wanted to study was not the classical or medieval law of India but the law that they believed was best suited to the times in which they lived. It was not just the attraction of lucrative careers that took them to the study of the law, but also the possibilities of social and political change that were offered by it.

It is remarkable how many of the leaders of the nationalist movement were trained as lawyers. They put this training to use in their struggle for both political liberation and social regeneration. The legal principles to which they took recourse in both causes were the new and not the old ones. Having mastered the basic principles of the laws introduced by the British, Indian lawyers found little difficulty in using those principles to turn the tables on their rulers. The leaders of the nationalist movement may have been very proud of their cultural heritage, but when it came to legal principles, they relied mainly on the ones that had been introduced by the British.

As they sought to apply the same principles for the regeneration of their own society, they found that the way ahead was full of snares and pitfalls. Large sections of the population continued to be in the grip of the old codes of conduct, whether we describe those codes as 'law' or 'custom'. Generally speaking, the old laws were more in tune with the old customs than with the new laws. What is more, those who wished to use the new laws for the regeneration of society were not themselves fully free from the old habits of the heart. Many of those who spoke and wrote eloquently in the cause of the rule of law were guided by the old codes of conduct in their treatment of women, of stigmatized castes, of bonded labourers, and many others.

The advance of the new legal order based on the rule of law was slow and uneven. The British wanted change, but they acted with caution so as to minimize resistance and disorder. Neither the British rulers of India nor their principal Indian adversaries, the leaders of the nationalist movement, wished to reverse the trend that had begun in the early nineteenth century or to restore the legal systems of the past. But the political aims and objectives of the two parties were very different.

When the Constituent Assembly met at the time of independence, the general consensus was to continue the task of building a new social order based on the rule of law. Without that, the task of building a nation on the basis of equal citizenship could not be seriously addressed. Dr Ambedkar took the lead in advocating the case for a modern legal order which he believed would be the only guarantor for democracy in India. When he said in the Constituent Assembly that the Indian soil was essentially undemocratic, he had in mind the retrograde customs inherited from the past.

Dr Ambedkar was criticized repeatedly in the Constituent Assembly for ignoring and disregarding India's traditional institutions and borrowing heavily from the Government of India Act of 1935 which was essentially a creation of the British. He held his ground and gave nothing away. He said: 'As to the accusation that the Draft Constitution has produced a good part of the provisions of the Government of India Act, 1935, I make no apologies. There is nothing to be ashamed of in borrowing. It involves no plagiarism. Nobody holds any patent rights in the fundamental ideas of a Constitution' (*CAD* 1989, VII: 38).

Dr Ambedkar was out and out a modernist, and he was not one who would hide his light under a bushel.

* * *

There was great enthusiasm over the new legal order created by the Constitution which its creators presented as a democratic as against a colonial legal order. The makers of the Constitution felt that where there were obstacles to the progress of the rule of law, they could be removed by legislation. They felt that freedom from colonial rule had greatly extended their capacity to legislate against rules and observances that were contrary to the rule of law as established by the Constitution. They felt free also to amend the Constitution to carry forward the task of building a nation in which all citizens would enjoy equal rights without consideration of birth, rank, or status.

But considerations of birth, rank, and status were the essence of the customs by which the lives of millions of ordinary Indians were largely, if not mainly, governed in the villages, and to a consider-able extent even in the towns and cities. When new laws created to advance democratic social and political objectives are obstructed by obdurate customs rooted in hierarchical habits of life and thought, fresh new laws may be enacted to remove the roadblocks. But the roadblocks have a way of reappearing in new forms at new intersections. Customs, unlike laws, are not generally created by legislation. Can they be abolished by legislation? Very often legislation does not abolish customs but only drives them underground.

It is of the essence of a modern legal system that it creates new laws by legislation in accordance with prescribed rules of procedure. Here lies the significance of the secondary rules described by Hart as essential components of a system of law. He calls the rules for creating new laws as rules of change and describes them as follows: 'Such rules of change may be very simple or very complex: the powers conferred may be unrestricted or limited in various ways: the rules may, besides specifying the persons who are to legislate, define in more or less rigid terms the procedure to be followed in legislation' (Hart 1970: 93). Plainly, we are very far from the rules of custom governed by immemorial tradition.

In modern democratic societies the making of new laws is a deliberate, systematic, and continuous process. There is a whole institutional apparatus whose principal task is to review existing laws and enact new ones. The legislature has emerged as a specialized and very important branch of the state. But it does not operate alone. The laws that it makes and authorizes other agencies to make are subject to review and challenge in the courts of law. The relationship between the legislature and the judiciary is a complex one with many ramifications that have been discussed earlier (Chapter 1 in this volume).

There are various reasons why the creation of new laws becomes a continuous process in modern democratic societies. As the rule of law brings more and more areas of social life within its ambit, the law itself becomes more complex and more differentiated. As the laws become more differentiated, the need for the integration of the differentiated parts grows apace. So in a sense, the creation of new laws leads to the creation of yet more laws. In our country it often happens that old laws remain on the statute books even after the creation of new laws has made them redundant or anachronistic.

The requirement of internal consistency in a moving system is not the only reason for the creation of new laws. What is more important from the present point of view is the use of legislation for the reform of society. It is here that law (or legislation) and custom come directly into confrontation with each other. This confrontation, when not handled with care, may lead to an erosion of confidence in legislation itself, and ultimately in the very institutions of democracy.

It is not at all my argument that custom never changes but remains for ever frozen in time. It is also not my argument that legislation can do nothing to change custom along lines considered desirable, and should therefore never be used for that purpose. But it is important to recognize that legislation has unintended consequences. Hence, some restraint has to be exercised against its wholesale use for the purpose of bringing about a radical change in the structure of society.

Society changes all the time through the operation of social and economic forces whose actions we do not fully understand. Changes in technology, in demography, in education, and in employment bring into being new social arrangements that gradually displace existing ones. When those changes carry society forward in directions considered to be desirable, legislation can give them an added impetus and make their action more effective.

We may take the example of the rules of marriage. A hundred years ago, particularly among upper caste Hindus, those rules were very different from what they are today. How did the rules change?

Did they change through the unaided action of legislation alone? Even a hundred years ago custom allowed the practice of polygyny and required a very low age at marriage for women. Public opinion began to change towards the end of the nineteenth century, but it did not change overnight or uniformly across all sections of society. The rules of marriage among the Hindus were drastically changed by the Hindu Marriage Act of 1955 which made the practice of polygamy unlawful and raised the age at marriage for women substantially.

The new laws did not change marriage practices at once, and violations of the law are by no means uncommon. Instances of plural marriages may be easily found, and marriages below the prescribed age are still widespread. But the tide seems to be turning. Public opinion is no longer acquiescent of the old practices to the extent to which it was even sixty years ago. Members of the educated middle class are turning their backs increasingly on the practices of their ancestors. This is significant for two reasons. First, the educated middle class is growing in numbers and will grow further, adding its weight to public opinion in increasing measure. Second, it is the upper castes, the erstwhile custodians of the old rules, whose members have turned most sharply against them.

Customs do change, and legislation can play a significant part in giving direction to the change. However, new laws can hardly be effective if those who enact them are unwilling or unable to track the changes in public opinion brought about by deeper currents of social and economic change. In a large and complex society such as ours, those currents do not all flow in the same direction, hence the difficulty of enacting laws that will be both progressive and effective.

A great deal needs to change in contemporary India. That is the general opinion among planners, policymakers, and public intellectuals. Public opinion is turning in favour of changes that will bring social practices more closely in line with what is prescribed by the Constitution and the laws. But public opinion in India is not unitary or organized. It varies with education, occupation, caste, community, and region. Public opinion in the educated middle class in the metropolitan cities is not the same as what may be called public opinion in the rural areas where *khap panchayats* and analogous structures of power prevail. Yet the tide is clearly turning against the worldview from which those structures of power draw their sustenance.

We have a good Constitution and we have good laws. But our laws are not as widely respected as they should be. They are often ignored or disregarded. The remedy for that does not lie simply in creating more laws. This holds true particularly for social legislation which cannot act effectively without a change in public opinion. Change in public opinion can be given added impetus by well-designed social policies. It is only when favourable circumstances have been created by such policies that legislation can be used to overturn customs that are beginning to appear more and more anachronistic in the eyes of those who are resolved to bring about change. Legislation by itself can do very little in the absence of favourable circumstances. For if it is true that men make their own history, it is also true that they do not make it just as they please but under defined historical and social conditions.

References

Béteille, André. 1998. 'The Conflict of Norms and Values', in Peter Berger (ed.), *The Limits of Social Cohesion*, Boulder, Col.: Westview Press, pp. 265–92.

Constituent Assembly Debates (CAD). 1989. *Official Report.* New Delhi: Government of India, vol. VII.

Dworkin, Ronald. 1984. *Taking Rights Seriously*. London: Duckworth.

Evans-Pritchard, E.E. 1940. *The Nuer*. Oxford: Clarendon Press.

Gluckman, Max. 1965. *Politics, Law and Ritual in Tribal Society*. Oxford: Basil Blackwell.

Guha, Ranajit. 1963. *A Rule of Property for Bengal*. Paris: Mouton.

Hart, H.L.A. 1970. *The Concept of Law*. London: Oxford University Press.

Maine, H.S. 1931. *Ancient Law*. London: Oxford University Press.

Malinowski, B. 1926. *Crime and Custom in Savage Society*. London: Routledge and Kegan Paul.

Nehru, Jawaharlal. 1949. *Speeches, 1946–9*. New Delhi: Government of India.

Pollock, F. and F.W. Maitland. 1968. *History of English Law*. Cambridge: Cambridge University Press.

Radcliffe-Brown, A.R. 1952. *Structure and Function in Primitive Society*. London: Cohen and West.

Stokes, Eric. 1959. *The English Utilitarians and India*. Oxford: Clarendon Press.

Tocqueville, Alexis de. 1956. *Democracy in America*. New York: Alfred Knopf, 2 vols.

Vinogradoff, Paul. 1905. *The Growth of the Manor*. London: Swan Sonnenschein.

9

Sociology and Ideology*

I would like to use this occasion to discuss the relationship between sociology and ideology. My view of the subject, which has been much influenced by the work of M.N. Srinivas, is that it is desirable to keep the two apart, although it has proved difficult, particularly in India, to insulate the practice of sociology from the demands of ideology. In what follows I will have something to say both about the justification for keeping the two apart and the difficulty of doing so in a clear and consistent way.

Those who wish to keep the two apart are obliged to explain, no matter how briefly, what they mean by sociology and by ideology. This is not an easy thing to do. Sociologists are by no means in complete agreement about the nature and scope of their discipline as an intellectual pursuit; moreover, their conception of the aims and objectives of sociology as a discipline may not correspond very well with their practices as sociologists. The concept of ideology has, if anything, an even wider range of connotations, and those who use it generally avoid giving it a clear or definite meaning.

Sociology, as I understand it, is an empirical and comparative discipline devoted to the systematic study of society through the

* This chapter was previously published in *Sociological Bulletin*, vol. 58, no. 2, 2009, pp. 196–211.

application of a distinctive body of concepts and methods, and here I would like to treat sociology as being inclusive of social anthropology. What I would like to stress at the outset is that sociology is an empirical rather than a normative discipline, although, as I will point out later, the relationship between value judgements and judgements of reality is a difficult subject on which there are considerable differences of opinion. The primary aim of an ideology is not to understand or interpret society, but to change it by acting politically on it. Sociology as an intellectual discipline does not have any definite or specific political agenda, but an ideology that did not have one would hardly deserve that name.

An ideology is normative, and not merely descriptive or analytical in its orientation. It is based on a particular vision of society, its past and its future, and it seeks to articulate that vision through a set of arguments about what is desirable and what needs to be done to bring it into effect. An ideology cannot be understood only in terms of its argument or its vision, however appealing or persuasive these might be. Ideologies seek to connect the universe of values with the realm of power, and make demands on the intellectual that are different from those made by science and scholarship (Béteille 1980).

The commitment of an intellectual to an ideology may take a weak or a strong form. In the case of most persons it takes a weak rather than a strong form, although there are intellectuals who have a natural inclination for expressing even a diffuse commitment strongly and forcefully, if not always cogently. Those who maintain or express strong commitment to an ideology tend to be drawn towards partisanship in the cause of a particular political platform or a particular political movement. Many believe, and I share that belief, that scholarship and partisanship make uneasy bedfellows (Bendix and Roth 1971).

* * *

It is not my argument that commitment to a particular ideology or even a particular political cause is in itself a bad thing. There are some who believe that ideological commitment in the cause of, say, nationalism or the class struggle, or feminism, provides an additional impetus to science and scholarship. I have known many natural scientists—physicists, geneticists, and others—who have maintained a lifelong commitment to one or another ideology or political cause while producing work of high quality as scientists. But the case is somewhat different with those whose scholarly work is in the human sciences. Ideological commitment does not impinge in the same way or to the same extent on the two types of intellectual activity.

The distinction between value judgements and judgements of reality presents itself very differently in physics and in sociology. In physics we do not ask what values objects in motion or at rest assign to their own actions. In sociology we can hardly avoid asking what values a person assigns to his own conduct and to the conduct of others in a given social situation. Where it comes to the study of fundamental particles or the genetic code, it does not matter very much whether the scientist is a radical or a conservative, a pacifist or a militarist. No special care is required to insulate the course of his research from his political commitments. It is a somewhat different matter when a Marxist studies disputes in an industrial plant, or a feminist studies conflict within the family.

We must take note of the ways in which sociology is like any other science and the ways in which it differs from the natural sciences. It is like any other science because it aims to arrive at a systematic body of knowledge whose validity can be tested by standardized procedures. It has its own concepts and methods, and its own body of data. A large part of sociological enquiry and analysis consists of the accumulation of new data to examine, criticize, and reformulate existing knowledge about society and its structures and processes. It cannot be equated with common sense which is limited, narrow, and often resistant to unfamiliar facts and conclusions (Béteille 2002: 13–27).

Sociology is different from the natural sciences because it deals with facts of a different order. These facts are not easily amenable to the kinds of tests to which the natural scientist is able to submit the facts with which he deals. Moreover, the concepts used in sociological enquiry and analysis are fluid and ambiguous. It has proved very difficult to eliminate preconceptions from the study of society and to replace them with concepts on whose meanings there is general agreement. This is partly because such concepts as family, class, and community carry strongly evaluative connotations for those who use them.

A book by a well-known German scholar on the origin and development of sociology is entitled *Between Science and Literature* (Lepenies 1988). It captures nicely the conflicting aims and tendencies through which the systematic study of society emerged in France, England, and Germany. The sensibility of the writer played an important part in this development. But this sensibility was regulated and channelled by the disciplined and methodical study of an increasing body of facts. We must never forget the part played by the controlled accumulation of facts in reaching a broader and deeper understanding of social life. Sociology would not be what it is without the development of new methods and techniques for the collection and scrutiny of facts. To be sure, the facts with which the sociologist has to deal have their own distinctive features, but he cannot take with those facts the kind of liberty that is allowed to the story teller.

Fidelity to facts imposes on the sociologist restraints of a kind by which neither the author of fiction nor the proponent of ideologies is generally bound. The ideologist is concerned less with society as it is than with society as it ought to be. His orientation, as I have said, is normative rather than empirical, and where different ideologies co-exist in the same society, disagreements among their proponents cannot be easily settled by an appeal to facts, for the same facts acquire different colours when they pass through the prisms of divergent ideologies.

The conflicting aims and tendencies which shaped the development of sociology left their mark on the thought and work of M.N. Srinivas. On the one hand, he was a strong advocate of the 'field view' which placed the sociologist under obligation to observe and record life as it was actually lived, without embellishment. In what he wrote on village, caste, and family, he was untiring in his effort to penetrate the myths that had grown around these institutions in order to reveal their actual structure and operation. He shared the scepticism of the scientist about all forms of received wisdom, and was acutely aware that the received wisdom about society, and that too one's own society, was much more difficult to dislodge than the received wisdom about nature.

While Srinivas was greatly attracted by the detached and dispassionate study of reality, he also realized that that kind of study could not be pursued beyond certain limits. He often spoke about the need for empathy in fieldwork, and the value of participation and not just observation for the collection of data. But while he recognized all of this, he also maintained that a line had to be drawn between sociological enquiry and social advocacy. For all his scepticism about the possibility for any individual sociologist to achieve complete detachment in his work, he was on the side of detachment as against advocacy.

* * *

The observation and description of facts does not complete the work of the sociologist. Another important part of it is to connect together the facts that he and other sociologists have collected. For this to be done effectively, the facts have to be collected according to certain accepted procedures, and the concepts used in describing and analysing them must have some general acceptance. All sociologists operate, explicitly or implicitly, with the notion of society as some kind of a system. But there is disagreement about the nature of that system, and, hence, about the approach best suited to its study.

The disagreement is clearly in evidence in the work of Srinivas's two great teachers at Oxford, A.R. Radcliffe-Brown and E.E. Evans-Pritchard. Although Srinivas's early training as a sociologist had been under G.S. Ghurye, his stay at Oxford between 1945 and 1952 had a great influence on his work (Béteille 2003). There he started his work under Radcliffe-Brown and completed it under Evans-Pritchard. Although he remained loyal to Radcliffe-Brown, I believe that in the end he found the work of Evans-Pritchard more congenial.

Radcliffe-Brown believed that a social system was a kind of natural system and that it was possible to create a natural science of society. That is the case he had made in his famous seminar at Chicago of which the text was published posthumously (Radcliffe-Brown 1957).

The same argument was made by him in the essays brought together by Srinivas and also published posthumously (Radcliffe-Brown 1962). If you regard the study of society as a natural science, you will find it difficult to accommodate any kind of ideology in its approach and method. While Srinivas never really warmed to the idea of a natural science of society, he was at one with Radcliffe-Brown in regarding ideology as an unwanted intrusion into the study of society.

Evans-Pritchard, who was Srinivas's other teacher at Oxford, gradually distanced himself from the view that social systems could be studied as natural systems or that there could be a natural science of society. His view of the subject was expressed in his Marrett lecture at Oxford at which Srinivas was present. In that lecture Evans-Pritchard (1962: 26) argued that social anthropology 'studies societies as moral systems and not as natural systems, that it is interested in design rather than in process, and that it therefore seeks patterns and not scientific laws, and interprets rather than explains'. Needless to say, there are echoes here of Max Weber's conception of sociology as a science of the interpretation of meaningful action (Sinnverstehendesoziologie).

The rejection of the view that sociology is a natural science does not mean that social facts cannot be studied systematically or that agreed procedures cannot be devised for their systematic study. Evans-Pritchard would maintain that ideology is an impediment to the study of society whether one views it as a natural system or a moral system. The student of society seeks to interpret the meanings that others give to their actions and not advocate his own values for adoption by them. Only, insulation from ideology poses additional challenges for those who regard societies as moral rather than natural systems.

Srinivas's two teachers at Oxford, Radcliffe-Brown and Evans-Pritchard, both used the concept of social structure in their analyses, although each formulated it in his own way. Srinivas used it extensively in his study of village, caste, and kinship. He felt that most prevalent accounts of these institutions lacked a proper framework for the presentation and analysis of facts. As a result, facts of different kinds were jumbled together, and value judgements and judgements of reality presented without discrimination.

*   *   *

Let me now return to the point that sociology is an empirical and not a normative science. As an empirical science, it is concerned with the observation, description, analysis, interpretation, and explanation of facts. It deals with a specific body of facts which we characterize as social facts. They are social by virtue of being general and collective. Explanations of social facts by an appeal to universal principles of individual psychology run into serious difficulties sooner or later. But the distinction between psychology and sociology, or individual representations and collective representations, is a complex and difficult topic into which I do not wish to enter here.

Speculation about the nature and forms of social life is as old as society itself. India has a rich and ancient civilization in whose intellectual tradition speculation and introspection occupied a central place. When we look back on India's intellectual achievements in ancient and medieval times, we are struck as much by its strength as by its one-sidedness. This is manifested in the continuous emphasis on formal intellectual disciplines and a corresponding neglect of empirical knowledge. There are great, not to say spectacular achievements in mathematics, grammar, logic, and metaphysics, but hardly any contribution to or even interest in such subjects as history and geography, if we leave aside what came with the Arabs.

This peculiar emphasis on formal as against empirical knowledge might have something to do with the social framework of the cultivation and transmission of knowledge in past times. The Hindu intellectual tradition was exclusive in more than one sense and to an unusual degree. Its bearers belonged to a particular caste, the Brahmins, and other members had a small part to play in the cultivation and transmission of systematic knowledge. Obviously, others also pursued knowledge and contributed to its growth in one way or another. But the traditional Hindu literati, who were the repositories of systematic theoretical knowledge, were by all accounts socially far more exclusive than their European or Chinese or even Islamic counterparts.

A tightly closed intellectual stratum, acutely conscious of the continuity of its own tradition, develops its own intellectual style. What is described as scholasticism had a luxuriant growth in India. Observers through the ages commented on the inward-looking character of the bearers of the Indian intellectual tradition and on their overweening conceit. The Arab scholar al-Biruni, who was in India in the early part of the eleventh century, was baffled by his encounter with the local pundits. They were supremely self-confident and treated him with great condescension. When he tried to bring some of his own knowledge to their attention, they refused to believe that he could have acquired that knowledge on his own or from anyone but a Brahmin pundit.

The overvaluation of theoretical knowledge or knowledge acquired through ratiocination, above empirical knowledge, or knowledge acquired through observation, remains a feature of brahminical culture to this day. This may be illustrated with an example from my own fieldwork in a village in Thanjavur district with a community of Brahmins. After spending some months recording observations on the domestic rituals of the Brahmins, I decided to shift my attention to the non-Brahmins in the village. I mentioned the matter to an influential Brahmin resident who had been of much help to me and whose counsel I valued. He told me calmly that I need not seek out any non-Brahmin informants for he would himself tell me whatever I wanted to know about their religious observances; and if that did not satisfy me, he would ask the most knowledgeable Brahmin in the village to answer whatever questions remained. I explained to him that what I wanted was to make my observations and secure my information at first hand. He said that he knew all that very well, but the non-Brahmins, being peasants, not only did not understand their own rituals but would lack the capacity to describe them to me in a coherent way. Not only that, he took the same view of the facts relating to agriculture. The non-Brahmins might practise agriculture, but the Brahmins alone knew the theory of it, and it was the theory that counted rather than the practice.

It is in this context that we have to understand Srinivas's tireless advocacy of the 'field view' as against the 'book view' of Indian society. For him, the field view of society represented the reality on the ground and constituted the core of the sociological approach. The book view, on the other hand, was based on readings of the classical and medieval texts which provided representations of social institutions from which the reality on the ground often diverged considerably. Srinivas was acutely conscious of the fact that the adoption of the field view in place of the book view meant a departure from the intellectual tradition he had inherited from the past.

Appreciation of the importance of facts for the systematic and comparative study of societies has led to the development and expansion of exact and reliable methods of data collection. The sociologist or social anthropologist who sets out to study any aspect of Indian society now has at his disposal a much larger body of facts than was available to earlier generations of scholars. Arguments about the nature and operation of social institutions no longer have to rest on introspection and speculation alone; they can be tested either by an appeal to the available facts or by the collection of new facts. The movement away from introspection and speculation towards observation, description, and analysis has been a movement from sociology as an amateur pursuit to sociology as a profession.

Attitudes towards the reliability and accuracy of data began to change as sociology began to grow as a profession. The change was more dramatic in social anthropology or the study of simple societies than in sociology or the study of complex societies. But sociologists and social anthropologists alike became more demanding about the quality and quantity of the data on which the analysis of social life was based. By the end of World War II, training in the collection of data became a requirement for entry into the profession. It is not that sociologists ceased to use official statistics or historical records; but they began to rely more and more on data collected by procedures they themselves devised and refined.

To the extent that sociology is both a discipline and a profession, the data collected by individual sociologists become a collective resource. The sociologist does not collect data only for his own use, but also for use by others. For this to be possible and effective, a certain amount of standardization of methods and procedures is required. Standardization is easier to achieve in survey research than in participant-observation, but this does not mean that those who collect data through intensive fieldwork or through case studies are free to do as they please (Srivastava 2004).

Whether they study their own society or some other society, sociologists, like human beings in general, have their own preconceptions, not to say biases and prejudices. It is difficult not to have any preconceptions on such matters as family, religion, and class. Ideological biases tend to creep in when one is not sufficiently alert to the demands of empirical enquiry. The shift from introspection and speculation to observation and description has been a significant step forward in creating awareness among students of society of the difference between value judgements and judgements of reality.

While it is desirable to exclude preconceptions from the systematic study of society, it is doubtful that they can be eliminated altogether. Observation and description are no doubt important in the study of society as it actually exists. But no systematic study of facts on the ground can get very far without the use of concepts. The question that arises then is about the extent to which we can formulate clear and rigorous concepts of, let us say, family, class, and community without allowing our preconceptions to enter into the very definitions we use of these phenomena. Here I would only say that as an intellectual discipline sociology requires a certain disposition of the mind among its practitioners. The sociologist has to keep an open mind about his concepts and be prepared to revise and reformulate them in the light of new data and of alternative formulations of the same concept by others engaged in the study of the same subject, irrespective of ideological predilections.

* * *

I do not wish to give the impression that sociologists themselves are in complete agreement on the relationship between value judgements and judgements of reality. There are disagreements both about

accepting the distinction in principle and making it operational
in practice. These questions have agitated the best minds among
students of society for a hundred years, and nobody really expects
to find clear answers to them that will be to the satisfaction of all.
What I would like to do here is to indicate some of the basic issues
by taking as my example the sociological study of religion. That
would be an appropriate example here because the first major work
by Srinivas (1952), *Religion and Society among the Coorgs*, has a direct
bearing on these questions.

Is there a distinctive sociological approach to the study of
religion? Religion itself has been a subject of study and reflection for
a very long time. The sociology of religion is by contrast a relatively
young subject. The oldest branch of study devoted to religion, and,
at least in the western tradition, by far the most important one for
centuries is theology. Then there is the philosophy of religion which
now occupies some of the ground held by theology in the past.
The philosophy of religion looks to theology on one side and the
psychology of religion on the other. We have also the very broad
and assorted body of work that goes by the name of the history of
religions. We finally come to sociology and social anthropology
which have also made religion a subject of their study.

The different approaches to the study of religion combine
empirical and normative components in very different ways. The
distinction between the normative and the empirical approaches is
seen most clearly in the contrast between the theological and the
sociological approaches to the study of religion. The theologian
is concerned primarily with questions of the truth and efficacy of
religious beliefs and practices. Such questions do not concern the
sociologist in the same way. His primary aim is to observe, describe,
interpret, and explain the ways in which religious beliefs and
practices actually operate. He does not seek to determine whether
the beliefs he studies are true or false, or whether the practices he
observes do or do not have the effects the believer desires or expects
them to have.

Religion and Society among the Coorgs is the first significant
sociological study of Hinduism made by an Indian; unfortunately,

few such studies have been made since then. It derives its sociological significance from the fact that the description and analysis are presented from the standpoint of the religious sceptic rather than the religious believer. It is empirical rather than normative in its orientation.

Srinivas's approach to religion was very different from that of the philosopher Dr S. Radhakrishnan with whose work he was familiar. He did not seek to expound the essence of Hinduism. As a sociologist, he did not treat religion as either completely autonomous, or as being eternal, invariant, and unchanging. Religious beliefs and practices vary and change, and this has to be viewed in the light of variation and change in the structure of society. No religion operates independently of specific social arrangements, and Srinivas set out to examine the two-way relationship between religion and social structure. He spoke of local Hinduism, regional Hinduism, peninsular Hinduism, and all-India Hinduism. He also showed how religious beliefs and practices were refracted by the structures of joint family, caste, and village. This kind of approach does not always find favour with the religious believer who is inclined to regard religion as pure, and society as corrupt.

The study of Coorg religion is sociological to the extent that it steers clear of any attempt to either extol or condemn Hinduism or any of its beliefs and practices. In my recollection of Srinivas in my early years with him in Delhi, he was inclined to poke fun at those who glorified Hinduism on the basis of some idealized conception of it, saying that they did not know what Hinduism really was. But then, he would not put up with any wholesale condemnation of Hinduism either. He once returned from a seminar, infuriated by a participant who had described Hindu beliefs and practices as 'mumbo-jumbo'. It is no easy matter to remain detached, objective, and value-neutral in the study of religion, and particularly of one's own religion.

There are two aspects of the sociological approach to which I would like to briefly draw attention. The sociologist does not study religion as a thing in itself but in relation to society and its other institutions. He acknowledges the great importance of religion but does not assign pre-eminence to it over all other aspects of society.

He does not dismiss religion as 'false consciousness', but at the same time does not subscribe to the religious interpretation of the world as a whole.

The second aspect of the sociological approach is that it is comparative in its aims. This means that it addresses all religions and not just one's own religion, and tries to treat all of them even-handedly. This is difficult, if not impossible, if the sociologist is committed to the values of a single religion and seeks to carry those values into the study of all religions. He is likely to do this unconsciously in any case, but must try consciously and methodically to restrain his natural inclination arising from his socialization within a particular tradition when he undertakes a sociological study of religion or, for that matter, any sociological study.

The sociologist's obligation to be even-handed and value-neutral in the study of religion is particularly important in a country like India where different religions with different world views and ideologies co-exist and are allowed and encouraged to grow and flourish. The comparative study of religion becomes difficult where studies of religious beliefs and practices become divided among sociologists according to their religious identities so that Hinduism is studied only by Hindus, Islam only by Muslims, and Christianity only by Christians.

*   *   *

I would now like to examine very briefly whether the argument that I have made in favour of detachment, objectivity, and value-neutrality can be extended from the field of religion to other fields of sociological enquiry and analysis. In my experience, many of those who are prepared to go along with the insulation of the study of religion from value judgements are not prepared to do so in the case of politics. These are mainly secular intellectuals who believe in the primacy of politics over religion, a belief to which, as a sociologist, I find it difficult to subscribe.

The most sustained and penetrating opposition to the separation of facts and values may be found in the Marxist tradition of social enquiry and analysis. Although that tradition has lost many of its adherents in the West, partly as a result of the failure of the Soviet experiment, it continues to have an appeal in India and other countries in Asia, Africa, and Latin America. In countries marked by acute economic and social problems, many continue to find inspiration in the ringing words of the *Theses on Feuerbach*: 'The philosophers have only *interpreted* the world, in various ways; the point is to *change* it.' Those who have a definite agenda for such change are generally inclined towards the use of political power for bringing it about. This is known in philosophical parlance as the dialectical unity of theory and practice.

The work of Marx provided a great inspiration for the sociological study of economic life. Marx sought to develop a distinctive approach in which social structure, social conflict, and social change were interlinked in such a way that they could be understood only in terms of their mutual relations. A central place is occupied in it by social class; hence it is often described as the 'class approach'. The Marxian approach, as developed by Lenin and others among his followers, adopts a distinct conception of class which in its turn cannot be understood except in terms of a distinctive social theory and a distinctive political practice.

The approach indicated earlier has been described as a dialectical approach, by which is meant an approach based on the movement towards unity of subject and object. The working class begins as the object of history, but in course of time becomes its subject or principal agent. This is the process whereby the proletariat, from being a class in itself, becomes a class for itself. The study of class is also a study of class consciousness, and class and class consciousness can be understood best by those who participate in their formation. The political practice through which this has to take place is not a distraction from the understanding of class but an essential part of it. In the view of Marx and his followers, only those who engage consciously and actively in the process of class formation can understand the real nature and significance of class.

The 'class approach' is not the only approach that follows the path of commitment and engagement for the understanding and analysis of social and political reality. The nationalist approach, which puts nation above class, has a family resemblance with Marxism in the demands it makes from students of society and history. The nationalist too seeks to understand the nation and its identity and unity, but the understanding he seeks is not that of the detached or disinterested bystander. Nation-building is a continuous process that is never completed, and the nationalist intellectual believes that only he who contributes to the process from the inside can expect to understand its true nature and significance. In a country such as India, there are many forms of sub-nationalism that make similar demands on their protagonist; needless to say, such demands sometimes act against each other and against those of nationalism itself.

Several new branches of social enquiry and analysis have emerged that also question the justification for separating value judgements from judgements of reality. They include gender studies, Dalit studies, and minority studies. These studies have sought to introduce new forms of discourse that are different in many ways from the discourse of academic social science. They impinge on one or more of the established academic disciplines, but also cut across them. Although they have emerged relatively recently, they have found accommodation in the universities and have begun to influence teaching and research in such subjects as sociology and social anthropology.

Among the fields that I have just mentioned, gender studies is perhaps the oldest and the most widely recognized. It has grown in response to women's movements in the different parts of the world. It is not that the position of women did not receive any attention in the past. Evans-Pritchard (1965) published a collection of essays with the title *The Position of Women in Primitive Societies and Other Essays* more than forty years ago, and Srinivas (2002: 279–300) himself chose the subject of 'The Changing Position of Indian Women' for his Huxley Memorial Lecture in the mid-1970s. But the emergence of women's movements has given the subject a new intellectual focus and new political energy.

The conditions of their origin and growth have been such that gender studies are largely in the care of women, Dalit studies in the care of Dalits, and minority studies in the care of minorities. In this respect the class approach is different. Although the proletariat is at the centre of its attention, it has been created and developed, from Marx's time down to our own, by members of the middle class and not the working class. However, that approach has provided political as well as intellectual inspiration to all emancipationist movements, whether of women or of Dalits or of the minorities. In that sense, the work of Marx has been 'equivocal and inexhaustible' (Aron 1970: 355–77).

* * *

I have tried to explain the nature of sociology as an empirical discipline which aims at the systematic and comparative study of societies, and to distinguish sociology defined in that way from ideologies that are systems of idea driven by more or less definite political objectives. I have also indicated how the practice of sociology is influenced by ideologies whose aims are different from those of the former. Those whose objective is to develop sociology as an intellectual discipline in India today cannot wish out of existence the strong ideological currents to which many students of the subject are drawn.

I would like to return in the end to the question of the relationship between value judgements and judgements of reality. As I have emphasized, this is a difficult question on which serious, and perhaps irremovable, disagreements continue to exist among students of society.

Positivists, who view the systematic study of society in the image of the natural sciences, believe that the separation of facts and values is not only essential but can be successfully accomplished through the formulation of standardized methods and procedures. I believe that such standardized methods and procedures are very useful, but that they have their limitations and can carry us forward for some distance in the human sciences, but not nearly the same distance as in the natural sciences. An obsession with 'scientific method' has sometimes had a stultifying effect on the understanding of society and its institutions.

As against the positivists, there are those who advocate the dialectical unity of theory and practice. They maintain that the separation of facts and values is neither possible nor desirable, and that bringing the two together does not distort but enriches the understanding of society. This course of action has many attractions, but I have found it prudent to maintain a distance from it because I believe that sooner or later it leads to the subordination of sociology in the service of ideology.

It is the third view about the relationship between facts and values that I find the most attractive. This view was elaborated in a series of writings by Max Weber about a hundred years ago. It acknowledges both the necessity and the difficulty of consistently maintaining a separation between facts and values in the interpretation of human action. As Weber put it, 'When the normatively valid is the object of empirical investigation, its normative validity is disregarded. Its "existence" and not its "validity" is what concerns the investigator' (Weber 1949: 39). But then he had also said: 'Nor need I discuss further whether the distinction between empirical statements of fact and value-judgements is "difficult" to make. It is' (Ibid.: 9).

Because the study of society and its institutions requires close attention to the values of other persons of which one may approve or disapprove, implicitly if not explicitly, it is important to recognize that the standpoint from which a sociologist makes his study affects the course of that study. No single sociologist can study society from every possible standpoint. Experience shows that two persons who examine the same social facts from two different standpoints tend to reach somewhat different conclusions. These different conclusions need not be contradictory; they may be complementary. It requires a special effort of will and of sympathy to reach a kind of reflective equilibrium between such conclusions when they are divergent. To repeat what I have said in another context, 'Where the same subject is being studied, and must be studied, by persons in different existential situations, very little progress can be made without candour about one's own views and consideration for the views of others' (Béteille 1987: 676).

The problem of reconciling studies from different if not divergent standpoints comes up again and again in sociology. I will end with one particular example because it is important in itself and because Srinivas gave much thought to it. This is the problem of the insider versus the outsider in the study of society. Srinivas acknowledged that the insider, or the person who studies his own society, enjoys certain advantages, but insisted that the outsider, or the person who studies a society other than his own, also has his share of advantages. He said:

> I must hasten to add that I am not only not against studies of a culture by outsiders but on the contrary *I am positively for them* ... There cannot be a single correct or all-embracing view. One view ought to be that of the insider and various views can be complementary even when—or specially when they differ from each other. (Srinivas 2002: 560, emphasis in original)

The practice of sociology and social anthropology in India has taught us that keeping an open mind is of the highest importance, and it is this that is threatened by a zealous commitment to an ideology. It has taught us that there is no one unique or privileged standpoint in the study of society and culture. Even within the same society there generally is a plurality of standpoints, varying with religion, class, gender, or moral and intellectual predilection, and, besides, different outsiders may view the same society from different standpoints. Sociology and social anthropology cannot move forward unless the plurality of standpoints is accepted as a fundamental condition for the systematic and comparative study of society and culture. But it is one thing to acknowledge the value of, say, studying marriage from the standpoint of a woman, or discrimination from that of a Dalit, and quite another to have the standpoint itself defined by a particular political agenda.

References

Aron, Raymond. 1970. *Marximes imaginaires*. Paris: Gallimard.

Bendix, Reinhard and Guenther Roth. 1971. *Scholarship and Partisanship*. Berkeley: University of California Press.

Béteille, André. 1980. *Ideologies and Intellectuals*. New Delhi: Oxford University Press.

————. 1987. 'On Individualism and Equality', *Current Anthropology*, vol. 28, no. 5, pp. 672–6.

————. 2002. *Sociology*. New Delhi: Oxford University Press.

————. 2003. 'Introduction to the New Impression', in M.N. Srinivas, *Religion and Society among the Coorgs*, New Delhi: Oxford University Press, pp. xvii–xxix.

Evans-Pritchard, E.E. 1962. *Essays in Social Anthropology*. London: Faber & Faber.

————. 1965. *The Position of Women in Primitive Societies and Other Essays*. London: Faber & Faber.

Lepenies, Wolf. 1988. *Between Science and Literature*. Cambridge: Cambridge University Press.

Radcliffe-Brown, A.R. 1957. *A Natural Science of Society*. Glencoe: Free Press.

————. 1962. *Method in Social Anthropology*. Bombay: Asia Publishing House.

Srinivas, M.N. 1952. *Religion and Society among the Coorgs*. Oxford: Clarendon Press.

————. 2002. *Collected Essays*. New Delhi: Oxford University Press.

Srivastava, Vinay Kumar (ed.). 2004. *Methodology and Fieldwork*. New Delhi: Oxford University Press.

Weber, Max. 1949. *The Methodology of the Social Sciences*. New York: Free Press.

Index